[illegible] Phot[illegible]'s [illegible]uide TO LONDON

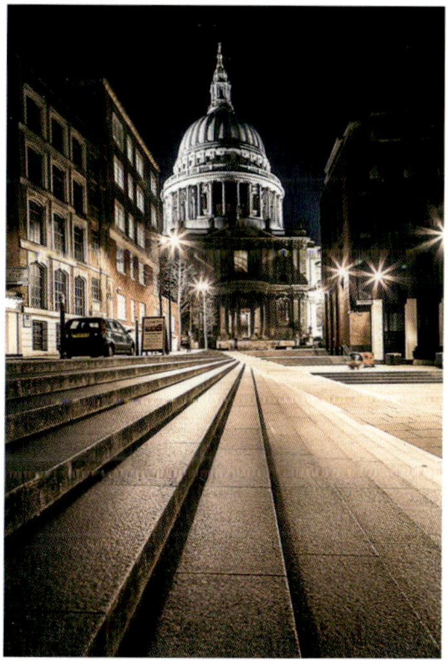

Long Valley Books

www.longvalleybooks.com

ISBN: 978 0 9926834 36

Published by Long Valley Books.

With thanks to Jane Ellingham for her help with proofreading and Neil Berry for his never ending support. I'd also like to thank all the photographers who have allowed me to use their stunning photos (see page 112 for details).

Every effort has been made to ensure the accuracy of this book at the time of going to print, however details such as opening times, entrance ticket prices and travel information are liable to change. Construction work may also cause closures of buildings and obscure some views. If you would like to report any errors please email info@longvalleybooks.com. Neither the publisher or author can accept any responsibility for any consequences arising from the use of this book, nor for any material published on third party websites.

Printed by MTP Media Ltd, Kendal.

Contents

SECTION 3» North London

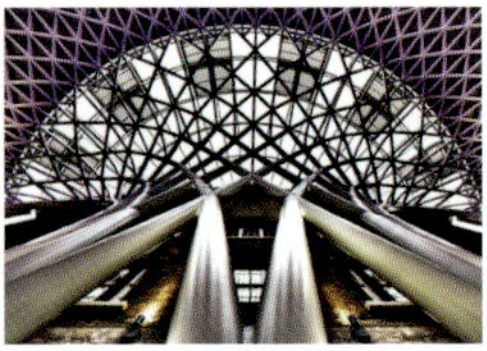

SECTION 4» South Bank, Bankside & Southwark

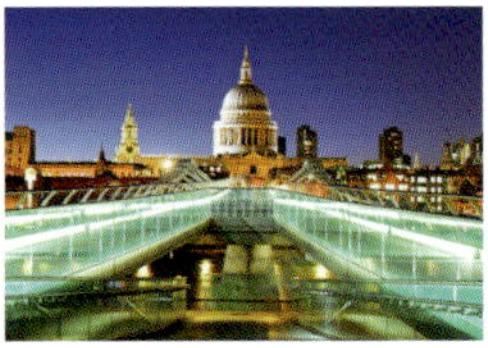

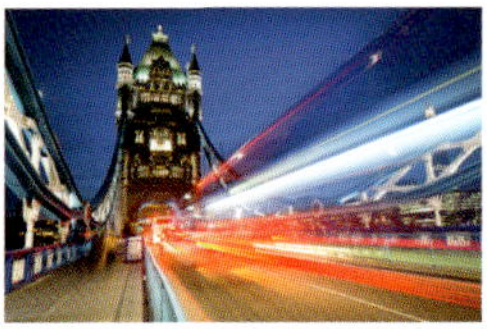

SECTION 5» The City

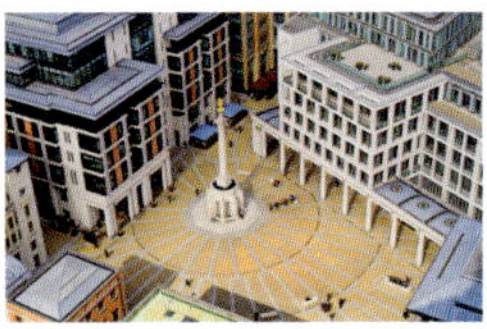

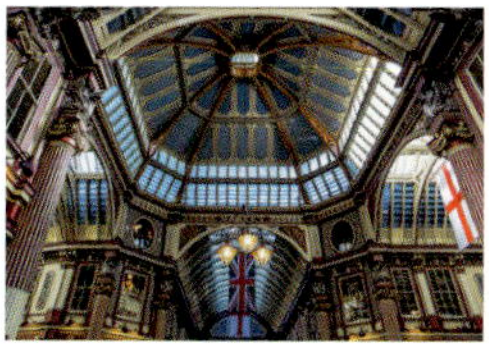

SECTION 6» Docklands & Greenwich

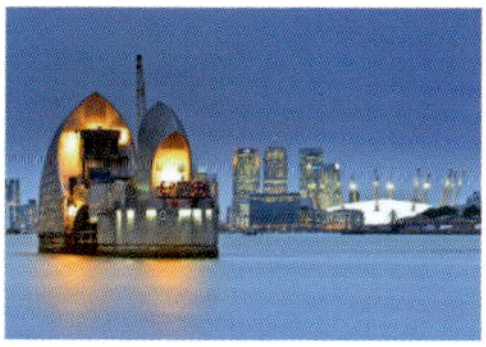

Introduction

London is of one of the world's most photogenic cities and is packed with stunning locations, from skyscrapers, historic buildings and bridges to museums and markets. Whether you're totally unfamiliar with London and are visiting for the first time or you've spent quite a bit of time in the city already, this guide will help you to choose where to photograph, when to photograph and what viewpoints are best to get that shot worthy of hanging on your wall.

It doesn't matter whether you're a beginner with a compact camera just starting out, or a seasoned photographer with all the kit — it's still just about getting out there and exploring the locations. This isn't a definitive list, as London is a very big city with many places of interest, but these locations are some of the best. There's also an extra section at the back of the book covering special interest locations, such as churches, parks and gardens.

I've given all the practical information you need for visiting each location, such as opening times, entrance ticket prices and travel information, but do be aware that these are liable to change and some locations may occasionally be closed for events. So if you're planning a special trip to a particular location it's best to check beforehand that it's open (phone numbers and websites are listed where applicable). All locations in the book are accessible by wheelchair, with the exceptions of 16, 36 and 37.

When you get to your chosen location I'd encourage you to scout around the whole area and find a composition that works for you, although don't be bashful about replicating the iconic shots you've seen many times... there's a reason they're iconic!

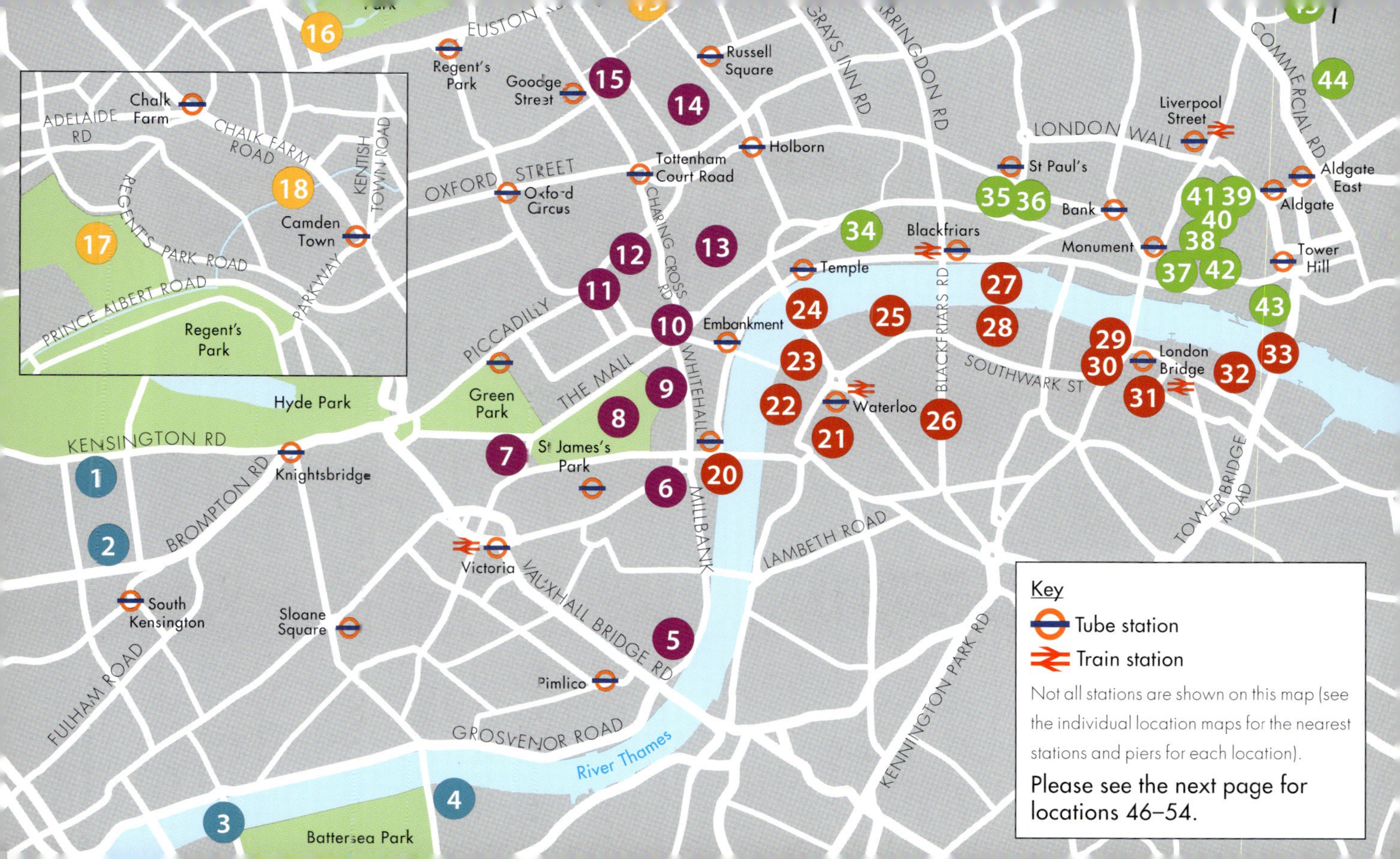
Key
Tube station
Train station
Not all stations are shown on this map (see the individual location maps for the nearest stations and piers for each location).
Please see the next page for locations 46–54.
Chalk Farm
Adelaide Rd
Chalk Farm Road
Kentish Town Road
Camden Town
Regent's Park Road
Prince Albert Road
Parkway
Regent's Park
Euston Rd
Regent's Park
Goodge Street
Russell Square
Grays Inn Rd
Farringdon Rd
London Wall
Liverpool Street
Commercial Rd
Aldgate East
Aldgate
Holborn
Tottenham Court Road
Oxford Street
Oxford Circus
St Paul's
Bank
Monument
Tower Hill
Blackfriars
Temple
Charing Cross Rd
Piccadilly
Embankment
Green Park
The Mall
Whitehall
Hyde Park
Kensington Rd
Knightsbridge
St James's Park
Brompton Rd
Millbank
Blackfriars Rd
Southwark St
Waterloo
London Bridge
Tower Bridge Road
Lambeth Road
Victoria
Vauxhall Bridge Rd
South Kensington
Sloane Square
Fulham Road
Pimlico
Grosvenor Road
River Thames
Kennington Park Rd
Battersea Park
1
2
3
4
5
6
7
8
9
10
11
12
13
14
15
16
17
18
20
21
22
23
24
25
26
27
28
29
30
31
32
33
34
35
36
37
38
39
40
41
42
43
44

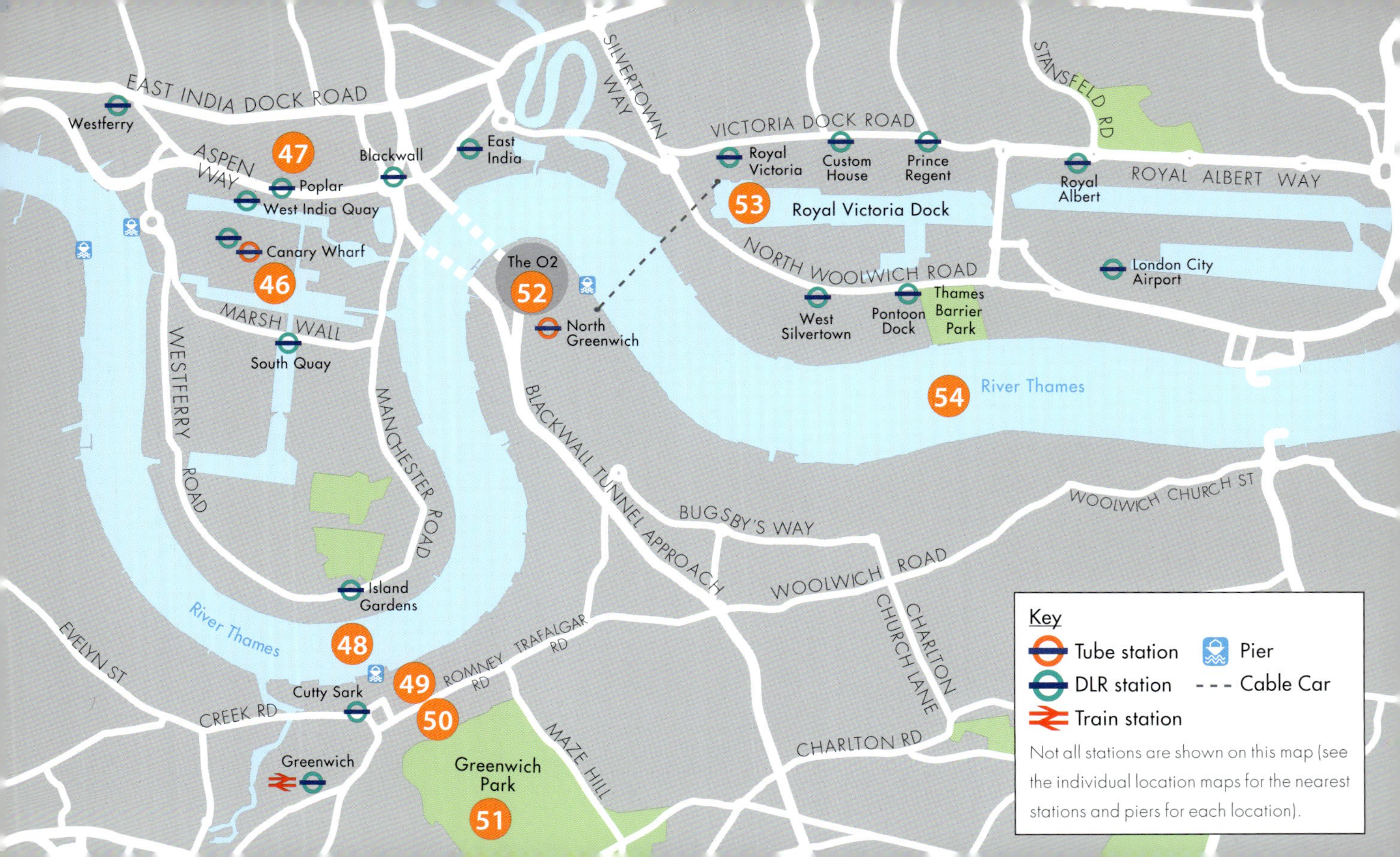

EAST INDIA DOCK ROAD
Westferry
47
ASPEN WAY
Poplar
West India Quay
Canary Wharf
46
Blackwall
East India
MARSH WALL
South Quay
WESTFERRY ROAD
MANCHESTER ROAD
Island Gardens
River Thames
48
Cutty Sark
49
50
CREEK RD
EVELYN ST
Greenwich
ROMNEY RD
TRAFALGAR RD
Greenwich Park
51
MAZE HILL
The O2
52
North Greenwich
SILVERTOWN WAY
VICTORIA DOCK ROAD
Royal Victoria
Custom House
Prince Regent
53
Royal Victoria Dock
NORTH WOOLWICH ROAD
West Silvertown
Pontoon Dock
Thames Barrier Park
STANSFELD RD
Royal Albert
ROYAL ALBERT WAY
London City Airport
54
River Thames
BLACKWALL TUNNEL APPROACH
BUGSBY'S WAY
WOOLWICH ROAD
WOOLWICH CHURCH ST
CHARLTON CHURCH LANE
CHARLTON RD
Key
Tube station
DLR station
Train station
Pier
Cable Car
Not all stations are shown on this map (see the individual location maps for the nearest stations and piers for each location).

1 SECTION West London

On the western side of central London are the districts of Kensington, Chelsea and Knightsbridge. These are some of the most affluent districts in London and the area is rich in Victorian and Georgian architecture. South Kensington is the main museum district in London and has two buildings that are notably photogenic – The Royal Albert Hall, which is best photographed at night, and the Natural History Museum, which has both a beautiful exterior and interior. Having said that there are many other buildings with beautiful exteriors in the area, such as the Royal College of Music and the V&A Museum (from the central courtyard). If you're in the area at night I'd also recommend checking out the famous department store Harrods (on Brompton Road) as it's lit by hundreds of bulbs and makes a great street scene with light trails from passing traffic in the foreground.

If you're interested in photographing parks and gardens, Hyde Park and Kensington Gardens are just to the north of the museum district, and Holland Park with its lovely Kyoto Garden isn't far away either (see pages 103–104 for more). If you're more interested in markets, the best one to visit in the area is Portobello Road Market (see page 100 for more).

To the south there are two great locations on the banks of the Thames – Albert Bridge and Battersea Power Station. Albert Bridge is very elegant and beautifully lit at night, although Chelsea Bridge is similarly lit so also worth exploring if you're in the area. Battersea Power Station has long been an iconic landmark on the Thames and there are a variety of different viewpoints to shoot it from.

Much further west of the central area are two of the best green spaces in London – Kew Gardens and Richmond Park (see pages 102–103 for more). Kew Gardens is a must-visit location if you're interested in botanical photography and Richmond Park is one of the best places in London for wildlife photography.

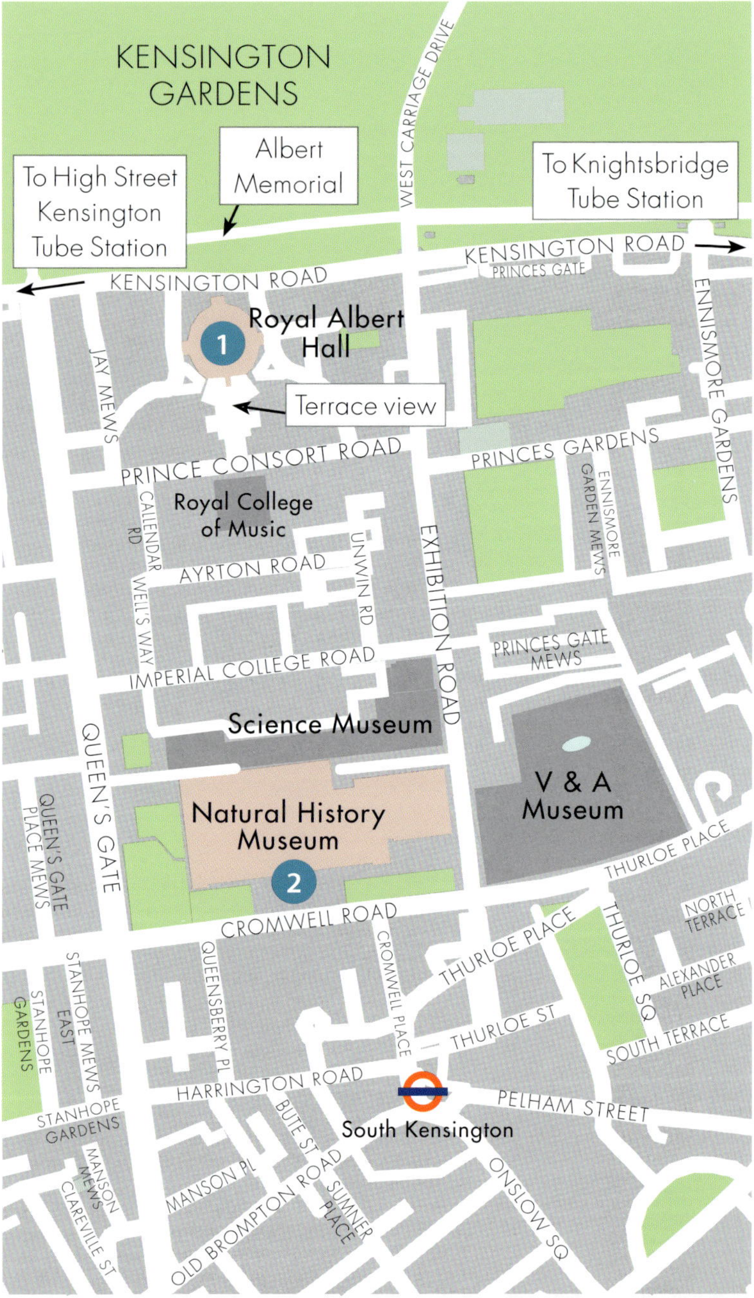
KENSINGTON GARDENS
Albert Memorial
To High Street Kensington Tube Station
To Knightsbridge Tube Station
WEST CARRIAGE DRIVE
KENSINGTON ROAD
KENSINGTON ROAD
PRINCES GATE
ENNISMORE GARDENS
Royal Albert Hall
1
JAY MEWS
Terrace view
PRINCE CONSORT ROAD
PRINCES GARDENS
ENNISMORE GARDEN MEWS
Royal College of Music
CALLENDAR RD
AYRTON ROAD
UNWIN RD
WELL'S WAY
EXHIBITION ROAD
IMPERIAL COLLEGE ROAD
PRINCES GATE MEWS
Science Museum
QUEEN'S GATE
V & A Museum
Natural History Museum
2
QUEEN'S GATE PLACE MEWS
THURLOE PLACE
NORTH TERRACE
CROMWELL ROAD
THURLOE PLACE
THURLOE SQ
ALEXANDER PLACE
STANHOPE MEWS EAST
STANHOPE GARDENS
QUEENSBERRY PL
CROMWELL PLACE
THURLOE ST
SOUTH TERRACE
HARRINGTON ROAD
PELHAM STREET
South Kensington
STANHOPE GARDENS
BUTE ST
MANSON MEWS
MANSON PL
OLD BROMPTON ROAD
SUMNER PLACE
ONSLOW SQ
CLAREVILLE ST

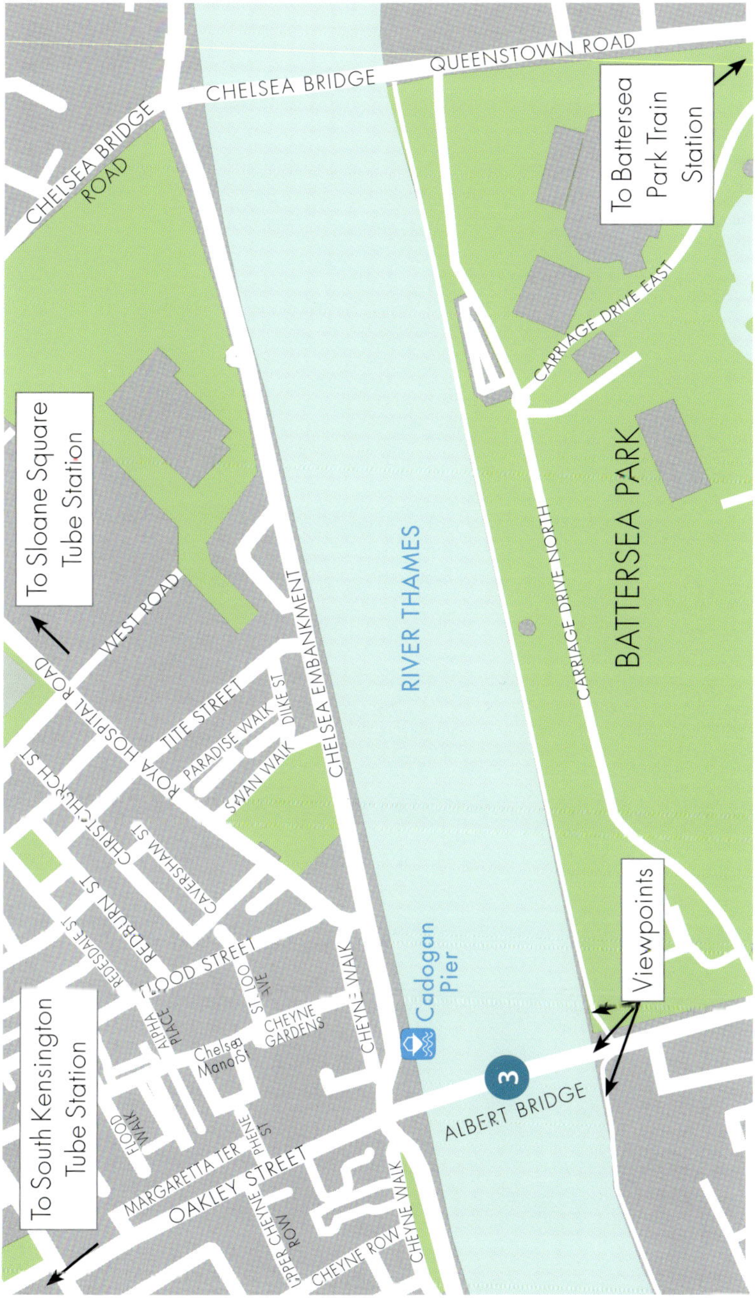

To Sloane Square Tube Station
To South Kensington Tube Station
To Battersea Park Train Station
Viewpoints
RIVER THAMES
BATTERSEA PARK
CHELSEA BRIDGE
QUEENSTOWN ROAD
CHELSEA BRIDGE ROAD
CARRIAGE DRIVE EAST
CARRIAGE DRIVE NORTH
CHELSEA EMBANKMENT
WEST ROAD
ROYAL HOSPITAL ROAD
TITE STREET
PARADISE WALK
DILKE ST
SWAN WALK
CHRISTCHURCH ST
CAVERSHAM ST
REDBURN ST
REDESDALE ST
FLOOD STREET
ST. LOO AVE
ALPHA PLACE
CHEYNE GARDENS
Chelsea Manor St
CHEYNE WALK
Cadogan Pier
3
ALBERT BRIDGE
FLOOD WALK
MARGARETTA TER
PHENE ST
OAKLEY STREET
UPPER CHEYNE ROW
CHEYNE ROW

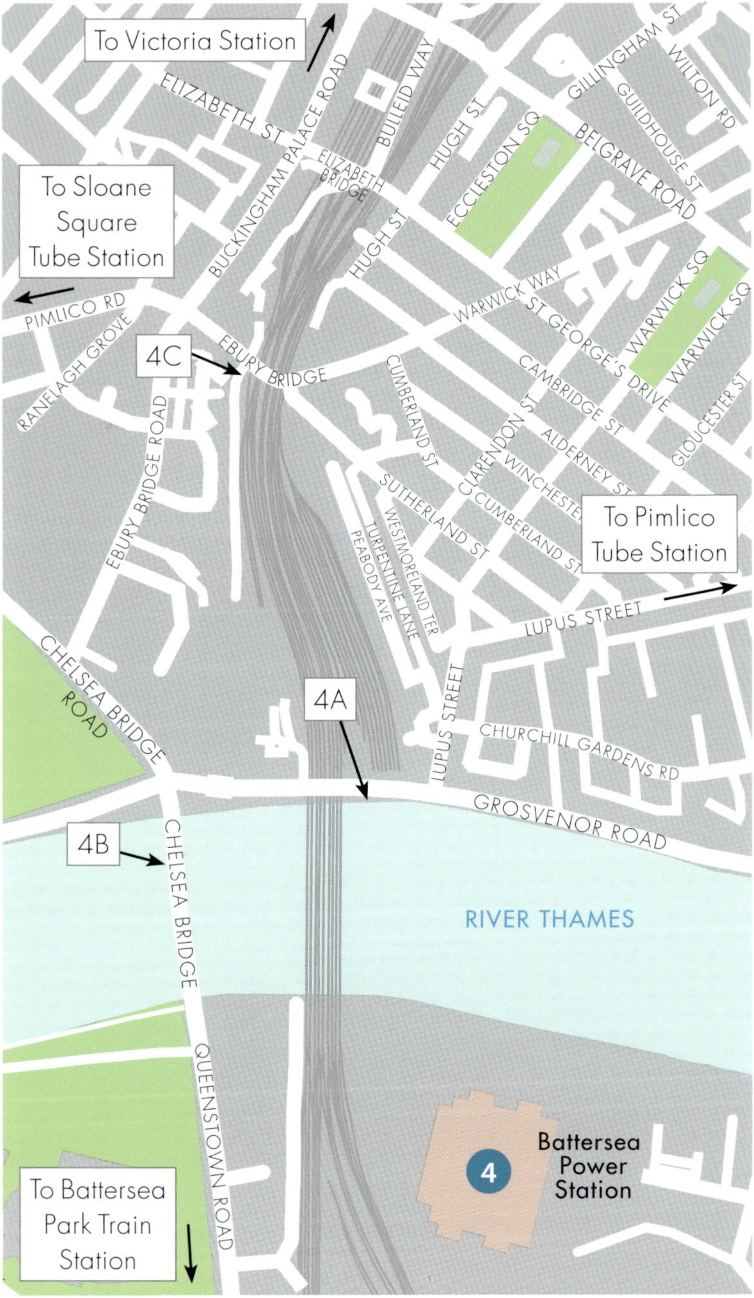

To Victoria Station
To Sloane Square Tube Station
To Pimlico Tube Station
To Battersea Park Train Station
ELIZABETH ST
BUCKINGHAM PALACE ROAD
ELIZABETH BRIDGE
BULLEID WAY
HUGH ST
ECCLESTON SQ
GILLINGHAM ST
WILTON RD
GUILDHOUSE ST
BELGRAVE ROAD
WARWICK WAY
WARWICK SQ
ST GEORGE'S DRIVE
GLOUCESTER ST
CAMBRIDGE ST
ALDERNEY ST
CLARENDON ST
WINCHESTER ST
CUMBERLAND ST
SUTHERLAND ST
WESTMORELAND TER
TURPENTINE LANE
PEABODY AVE
PIMLICO RD
RANELAGH GROVE
EBURY BRIDGE
EBURY BRIDGE ROAD
4C
4A
4B
LUPUS STREET
CHURCHILL GARDENS RD
GROSVENOR ROAD
CHELSEA BRIDGE ROAD
CHELSEA BRIDGE
RIVER THAMES
QUEENSTOWN ROAD
4
Battersea Power Station

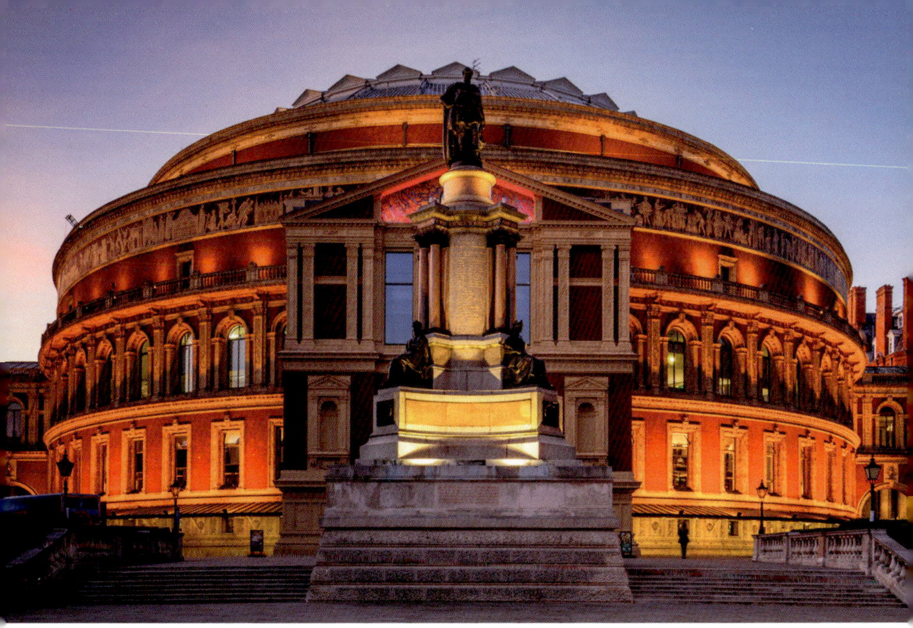

1 ROYAL ALBERT HALL

This concert hall opened in 1871 and has hosted music events of all types ever since. It's built of red brick with contrasting terracotta decoration and has a detailed frieze running around the top. The two best views of it are from the terrace on the southern side (pictured above) and from Kensington Gardens across the road on the northern side. These are both best at night, especially after rain as the reflections really add to the scene. On the northern side you'll also find the elaborately decorated Albert Memorial (pictured on the right), which looks great set against a blue sky.

» Practical Information

Tube: South Kensington, High Street Kensington, Knightsbridge

Bus: 9, 10, 52, 70, 360, 452

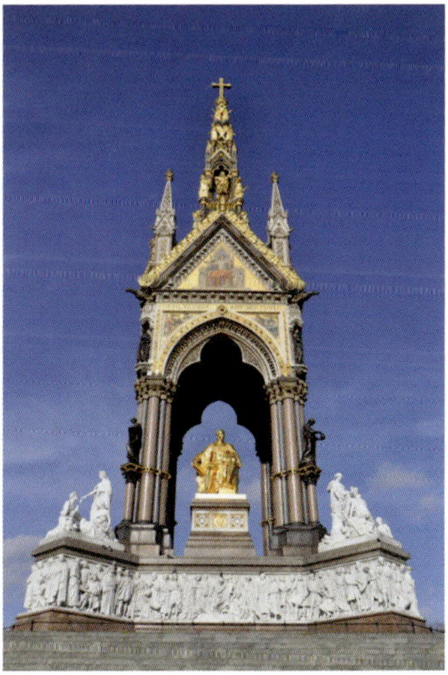

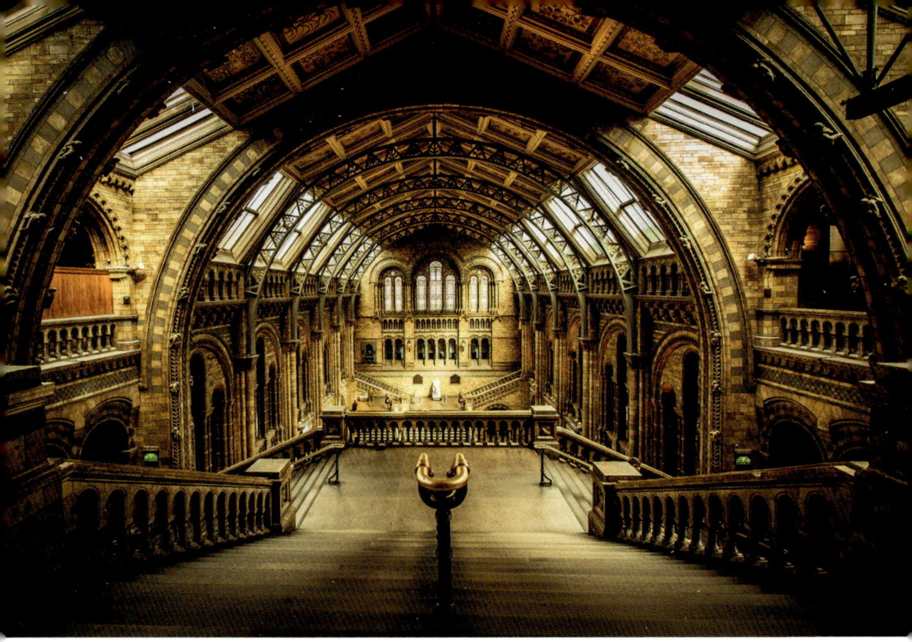

2 NATURAL HISTORY MUSEUM

This magnificent museum was built in the late 1800s and contains over 70 million specimens from the natural world. The ornate terracotta exterior is beautiful and lends itself well to close-up detail shots, especially of the arches surrounding the main entrance on Cromwell Road (pictured on the right). The inside is even more fabulous though, particularly the grand central hall. The hall is absolutely packed with detail – everywhere you look you'll find something of interest to photograph, such as the stained-glass windows, carved animals on the columns or delicate floral paintings on the ceiling. The two best places to take in the full scale of the hall are from the top of the staircases at either end (the view from the stairs above the entrance is pictured above). Tripods aren't allowed inside, but there are plenty of wide stone railings that make a good substitute.

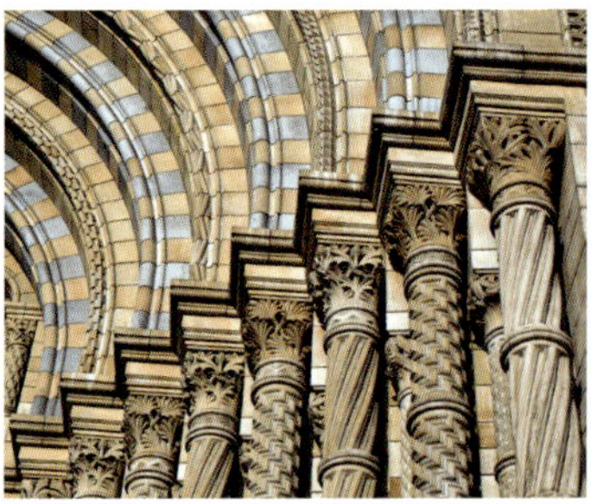

» Practical Information

Tube: South Kensington

Bus: 14, 49, 70, 74, 345, 360, 414, 430, C1

Web: www.nhm.ac.uk

Tel: 020 7942 5000

Open: 10am – 5.50pm every day (last admission 5.30pm)

Closed: 24–26th December

Admission: Free

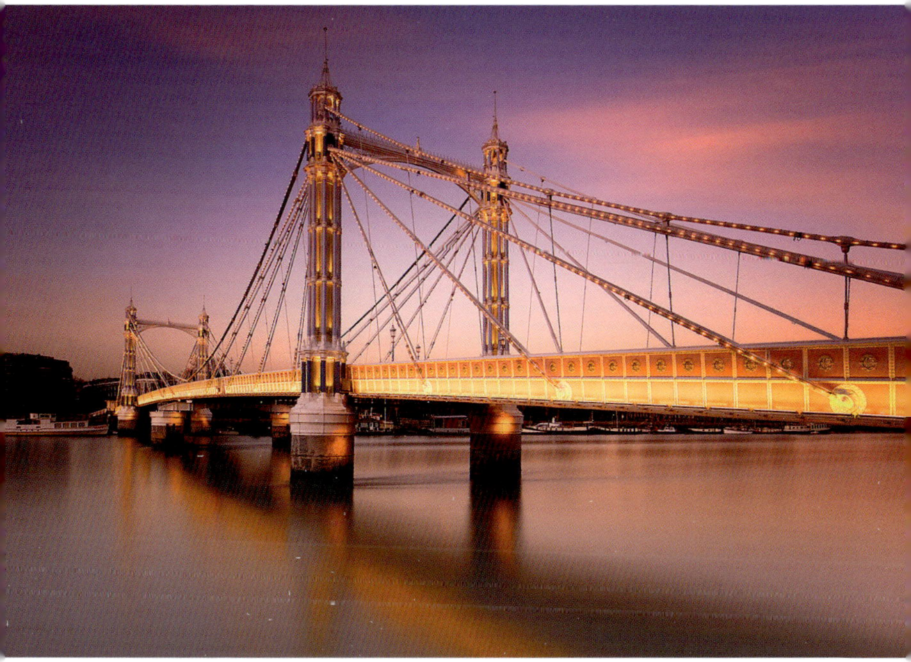

3 ALBERT BRIDGE

Albert Bridge links Chelsea on the northern bank of the Thames to Battersea on the southern bank. The bridge is a mix of styles, being part suspension bridge and part beam bridge. It's an unremarkable sight during the day, but at night it's lit by thousands of small lights making it very photogenic. There are three main viewpoints to shoot it from – the first is on the south bank, just to the west of the bridge (pictured above). There's a promenade that runs along the front of the river, giving you plenty of room to get a composition you like. Secondly, try from Battersea

Park on the eastern side, although trees make it a little trickier here. The third viewpoint is from the bridge itself looking straight along it (pictured below), which looks particularly good with light trails from passing traffic.

» Practical Information

Tube: Sloane Square, South Kensington

Train: Battersea Park

Pier: Cadogan

Bus: 170

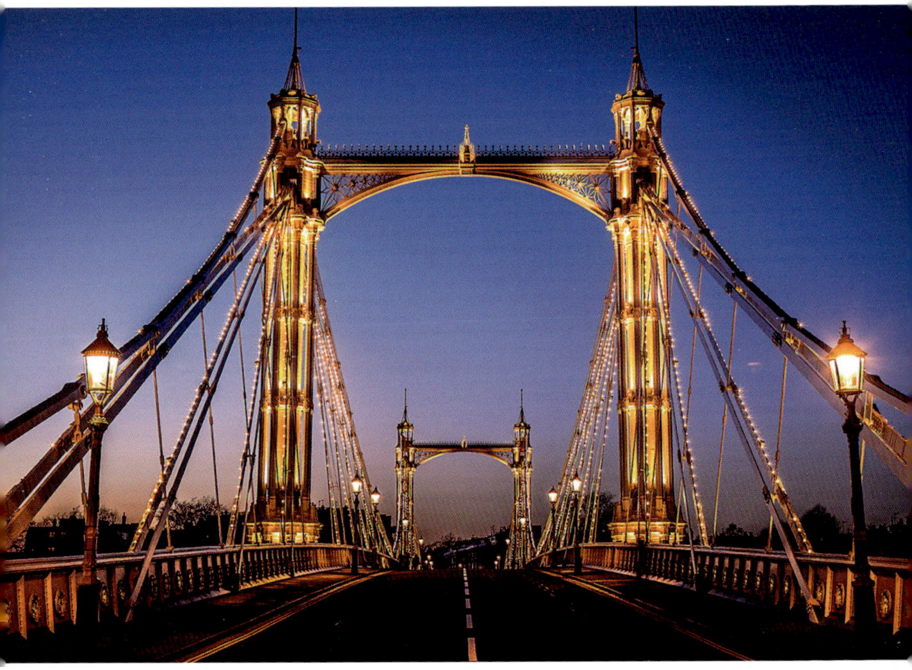

4 BATTERSEA POWER STATION

This decommissioned coal-fired power station is a well-known landmark on the banks of the Thames. The classic shot is from Grosvenor Road, where you get an uninterrupted view of the power station across the river with the distinctive white chimneys reflected in the water (pictured top right, point 4A on the map on page 7). A second good location is the northern end of Chelsea Bridge (point 4B on the map). From here you again look across the Thames, but this time with the Grosvenor railway bridge in the midground and the power station behind. Another good viewpoint is from Ebury Bridge, where the railway tracks going to Victoria Train Station provide a very interesting foreground (pictured below, point 4C on the map). All the locations are most attractive at night, although if you get a day where the Thames is still and there's a good sky viewpoints A and B are worth visiting.

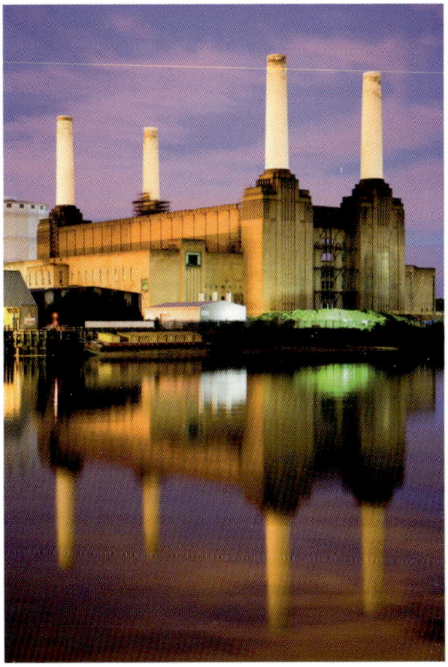

» Practical Information

Tube: Pimlico, Sloane Square (and Victoria for Ebury Bridge view)

Train: Battersea Park, Victoria

Pier: Cadogan

Bus: 24, 44, 137, 360, 452

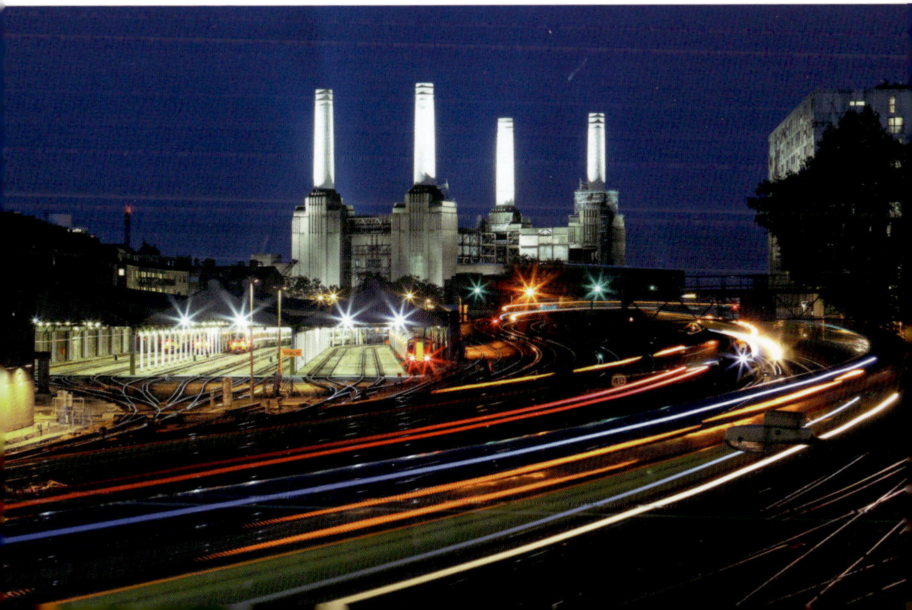

2 SECTION Westminster & The West End

The Westminster area is brimming with historic landmarks, such as The Houses of Parliament, Big Ben, Westminster Abbey and Buckingham Palace. They can only be photographed from the outside so I've included some of the best viewpoints to capture each one (though The Houses of Parliament and Big Ben are covered in Section 4 as most viewpoints of them are from the southern bank of the Thames.) If you're interested in royal ceremonies then you can photograph the Changing of The Guard at either Buckingham Palace or Horse Guards Parade, the latter being a mounted ceremony. Also in the area is the Tate Britain art gallery, which has a marvellous interior you could spend hours capturing.

Trafalgar Square is another great location, with Nelson's Column and The National Gallery being the main subjects of interest. It can be teeming with people during the day, so is often better to photograph at night. If you're there at night I'd also recommend investigating nearby Admiralty Arch (from the St James's Park side), as it looks great lit up and with light trails from traffic passing through the arches. If you're interested in church interiors it's also worth paying a visit to St Martin in the Fields Church, which is on the northeast corner of the square (see page 101 for more).

To the north of Trafalgar Square you move into London's shopping and entertainment district, known as the West End. There's a huge variety of subjects to shoot here, from museums to city life. Piccadilly Circus and Chinatown are excellent places to capture street scenes, especially at night when the neon signs are turned on. For street photography, Covent Garden is a great location as the mix of tourists and street-entertainers creates plenty of opportunities (another good location if you're into street photography is Trafalgar Square).

Not to miss for fans of beautiful interiors is The British Museum, which has a superb covered courtyard, but also an attractive exterior. Finally, there's a stunning spiral staircase I'd recommend visiting in the Heal's store on Tottenham Court Road.

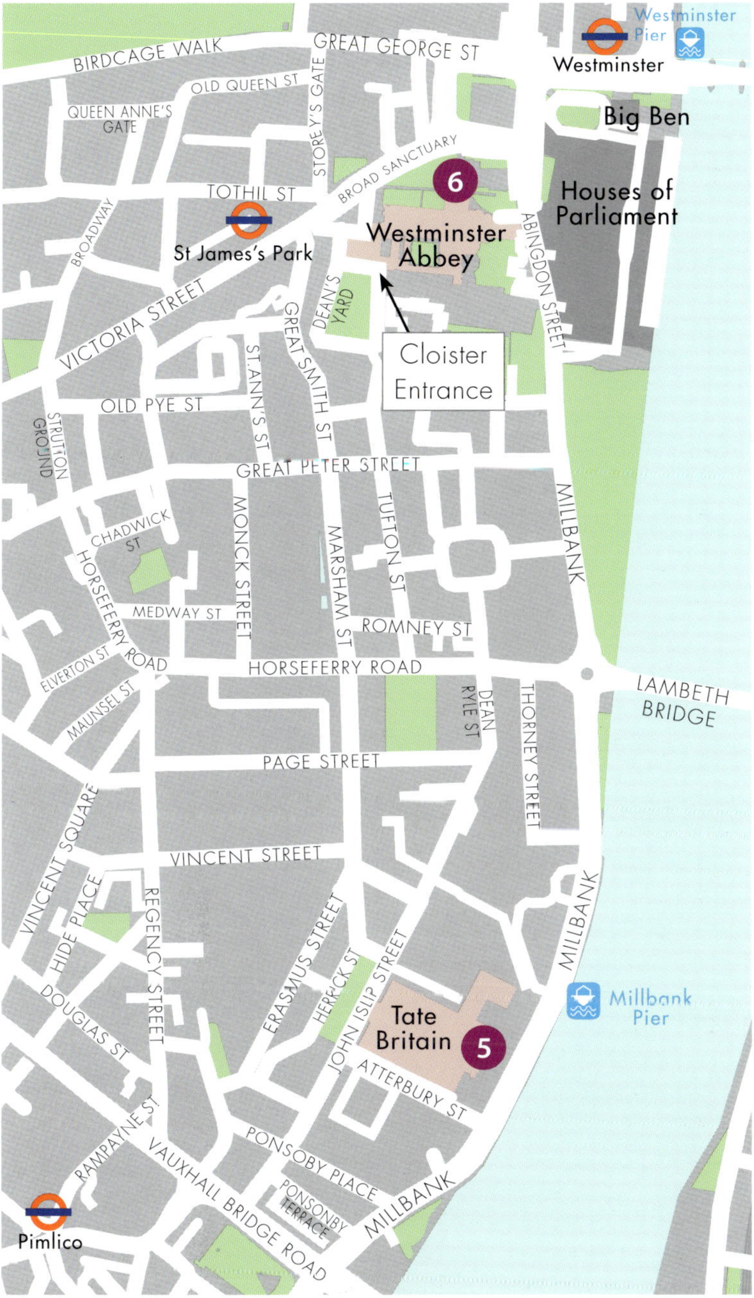
Westminster Pier
Westminster
Big Ben
Houses of Parliament
6
Westminster Abbey
Cloister Entrance
St James's Park
BIRDCAGE WALK
GREAT GEORGE ST
OLD QUEEN ST
QUEEN ANNE'S GATE
STOREY'S GATE
BROAD SANCTUARY
TOTHIL ST
BROADWAY
VICTORIA STREET
DEAN'S YARD
GREAT SMITH ST
ST. ANN'S ST
ABINGDON STREET
OLD PYE ST
STRUTTON GROUND
GREAT PETER STREET
CHADWICK ST
MONCK STREET
MARSHAM ST
TUFTON ST
MILLBANK
MEDWAY ST
ROMNEY ST
HORSEFERRY ROAD
ELVERTON ST
MAUNSEL ST
DEAN RYLE ST
THORNEY STREET
LAMBETH BRIDGE
PAGE STREET
VINCENT SQUARE
VINCENT STREET
HIDE PLACE
REGENCY STREET
ERASMUS STREET
HERRICK ST
JOHN ISLIP STREET
Millbank Pier
Tate Britain
5
DOUGLAS ST
ATTERBURY ST
RAMPAYNE ST
PONSOBY PLACE
PONSONBY TERRACE
VAUXHALL BRIDGE ROAD
Pimlico

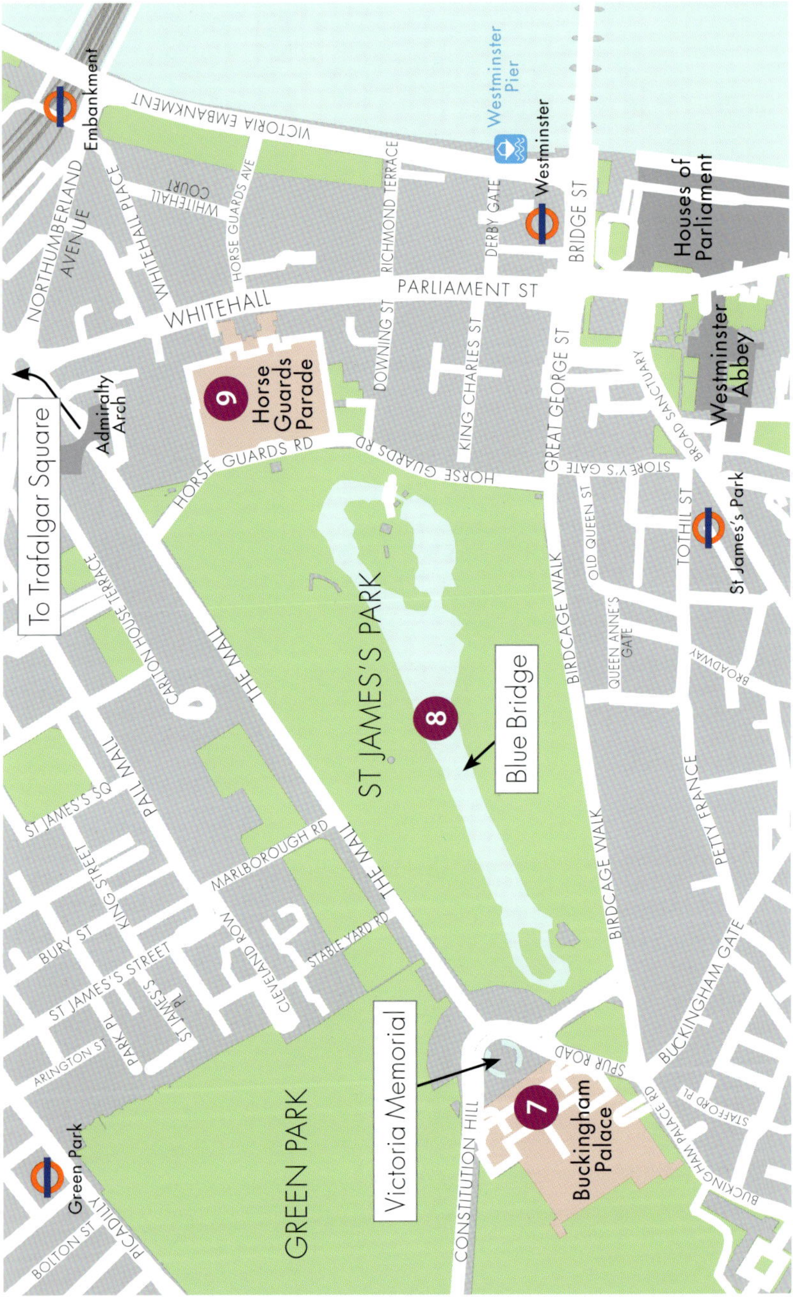

To Trafalgar Square
Embankment
Westminster Pier
Westminster
Houses of Parliament
Westminster Abbey
St James's Park
Green Park
9 Horse Guards Parade
Admiralty Arch
8
Blue Bridge
ST JAMES'S PARK
GREEN PARK
7 Buckingham Palace
Victoria Memorial
VICTORIA EMBANKMENT
NORTHUMBERLAND AVENUE
WHITEHALL PLACE
WHITEHALL COURT
HORSE GUARDS AVE
RICHMOND TERRACE
DERBY GATE
BRIDGE ST
WHITEHALL
PARLIAMENT ST
DOWNING ST
KING CHARLES ST
GREAT GEORGE ST
BROAD SANCTUARY
HORSE GUARDS RD
STOREY'S GATE
TOTHILL ST
OLD QUEEN ST
QUEEN ANNE'S GATE
BIRDCAGE WALK
BROADWAY
PETTY FRANCE
BUCKINGHAM GATE
STAFFORD PL
BUCKINGHAM PALACE RD
SPUR ROAD
CONSTITUTION HILL
THE MALL
CARLTON HOUSE TERRACE
PALL MALL
ST JAMES'S SQ
MARLBOROUGH RD
KING STREET
BURY ST
ST JAMES'S STREET
ST JAMES'S PL
CLEVELAND ROW
STABLE YARD RD
ARLINGTON ST
PARK PL
BOLTON ST
PICCADILLY

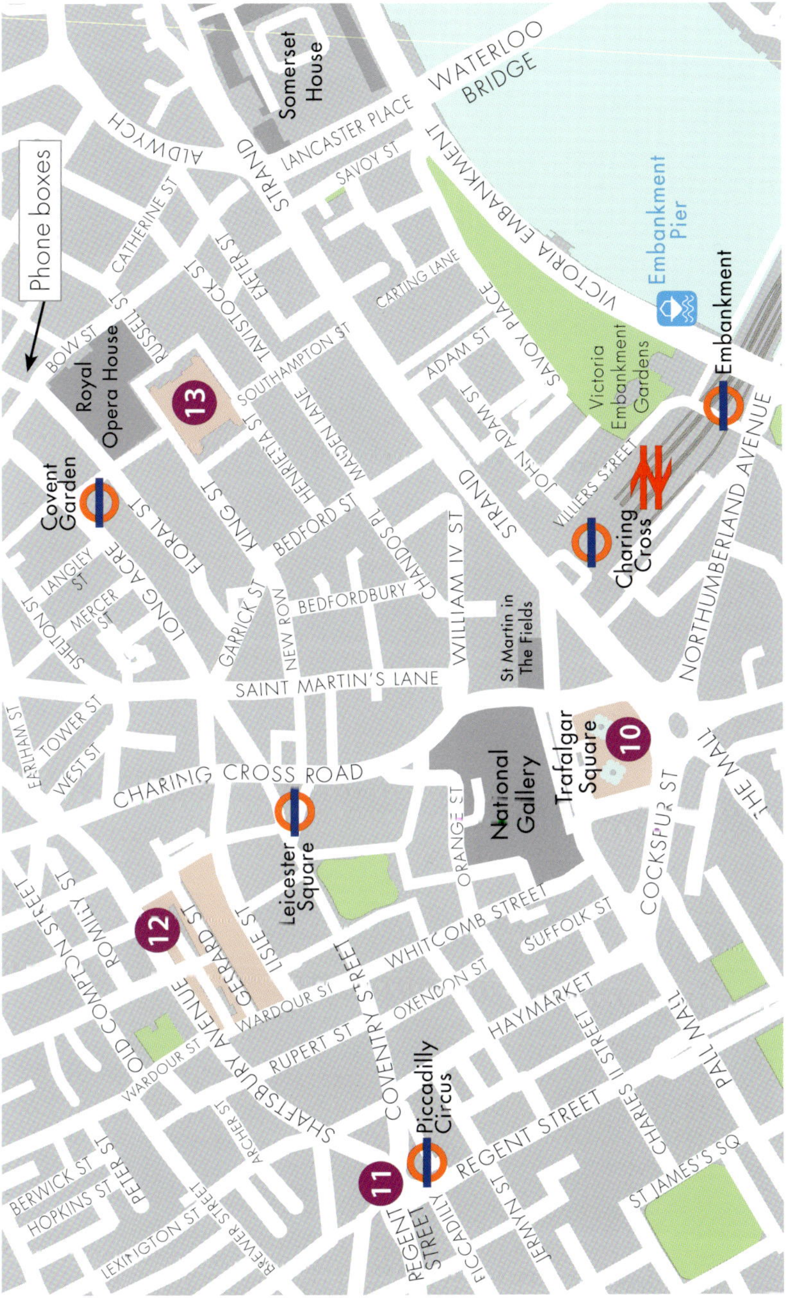
Phone boxes
Somerset House
WATERLOO BRIDGE
ALDWYCH
LANCASTER PLACE
SAVOY ST
STRAND
CATHERINE ST
Embankment Pier
VICTORIA EMBANKMENT
CARTING LANE
EXETER ST
TAVISTOCK ST
RUSSELL ST
BOW ST
Royal Opera House
13
SOUTHAMPTON ST
ADAM ST
SAVOY PLACE
Victoria Embankment Gardens
Embankment
JOHN ADAM ST
HENRIETTA ST
MAIDEN LANE
Covent Garden
FLORAL ST
KING ST
BEDFORD ST
CHANDOS PL
VILLIERS STREET
Charing Cross
NORTHUMBERLAND AVENUE
LANGLEY ST
LONG ACRE
MERCER ST
SHELTON ST
GARRICK ST
NEW ROW
BEDFORDBURY
WILLIAM IV ST
St Martin in The Fields
SAINT MARTIN'S LANE
EARLHAM ST
TOWER ST
WEST ST
CHARING CROSS ROAD
National Gallery
Trafalgar Square
10
THE MALL
Leicester Square
ORANGE ST
COCKSPUR ST
12
ROMILLY ST
OLD COMPTON ST
GERRARD ST
LISLE ST
WHITCOMB STREET
SUFFOLK ST
SHAFTESBURY AVENUE
WARDOUR ST
COVENTRY STREET
OXENDON ST
HAYMARKET
RUPERT ST
PALL MALL
Piccadilly Circus
CHARLES II STREET
REGENT STREET
ARCHER ST
BERWICK ST
HOPKINS ST
PETER ST
11
LEXINGTON ST
BREWER STREET
REGENT STREET
PICCADILLY
JERMYN ST
ST JAMES'S SQ

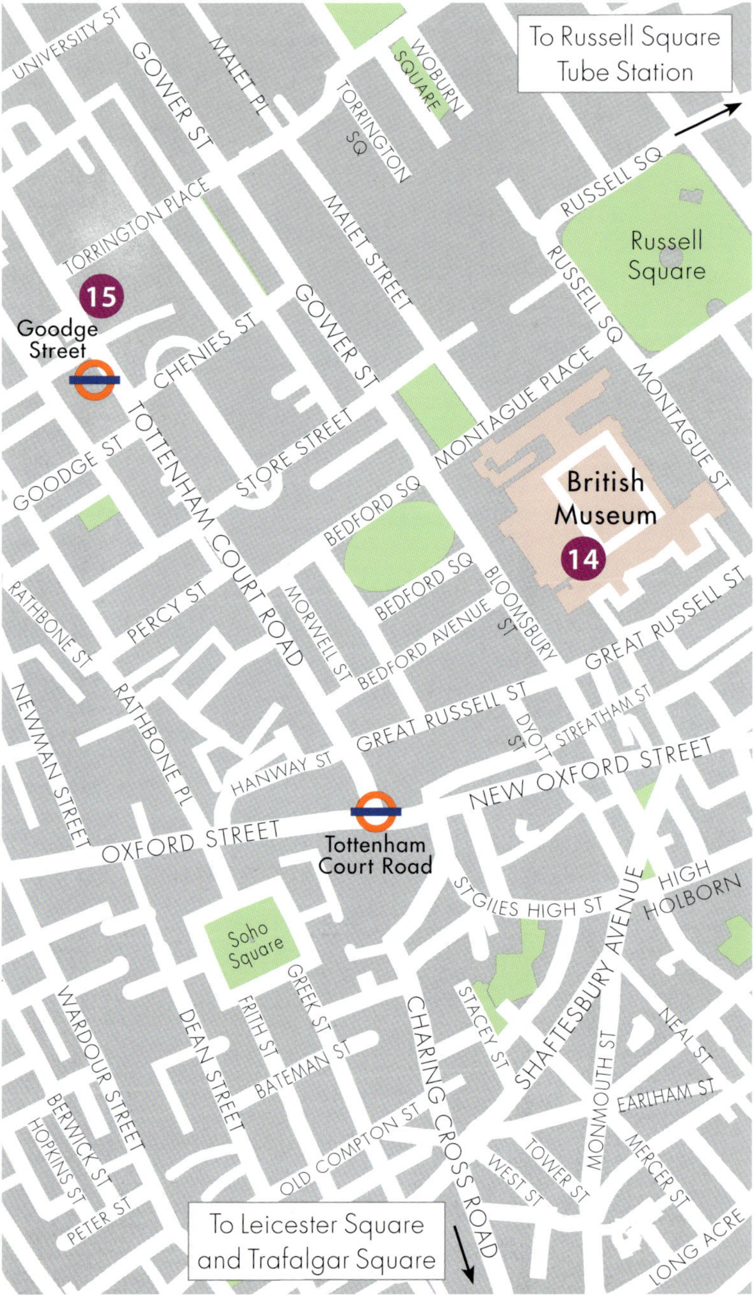
To Russell Square Tube Station
University St
Gower St
Malet Pl
Woburn Square
Torrington Sq
Russell Sq
Russell Square
Torrington Place
Malet Street
15
Goodge Street
Chenies St
Gower St
Montague Place
Montague St
Tottenham Court Road
Store Street
Goodge St
Bedford Sq
British Museum
14
Rathbone St
Percy St
Morwell St
Bloomsbury St
Great Russell St
Bedford Avenue
Newman Street
Rathbone Pl
Great Russell St
Dyott St
Streatham St
Hanway St
New Oxford Street
Oxford Street
Tottenham Court Road
St Giles High St
High Holborn
Soho Square
Greek St
Frith St
Stacey St
Shaftesbury Avenue
Charing Cross Road
Wardour Street
Dean Street
Bateman St
Monmouth St
Neal St
Earlham St
Berwick St
Hopkins St
Old Compton St
West St
Tower St
Mercer St
Peter St
Long Acre
To Leicester Square and Trafalgar Square

5 TATE BRITAIN

This art gallery has a wonderfully elegant interior with a variety of different subjects to photograph. Just inside the main entrance you'll find the Rotunda, which is a circular full-height room topped by a delicate glass dome. There's a small but stunning spiral staircase in the middle, which looks particularly good in black and white (pictured below). As well as shooting it looking down from the main floor try from the lower floor too, where you get a view of the foot of the stairs surrounded by archways and art deco lights. Using an archway to frame the scene also works well. It's quite dark on this level, so you'll need steady hands to shoot down here (unfortunately tripods aren't allowed in the gallery).

There's also another spiral staircase on the left as you come in the main entrance, which leads up to the Members' Room. (This area is only for Tate members, but the staircase is open to non-members.) It's taller and more minimalist than the central staircase, but again looks great in black and white.

Another feature not to miss in the Rotunda is the impressive dome. The classic view of it is from the main floor looking

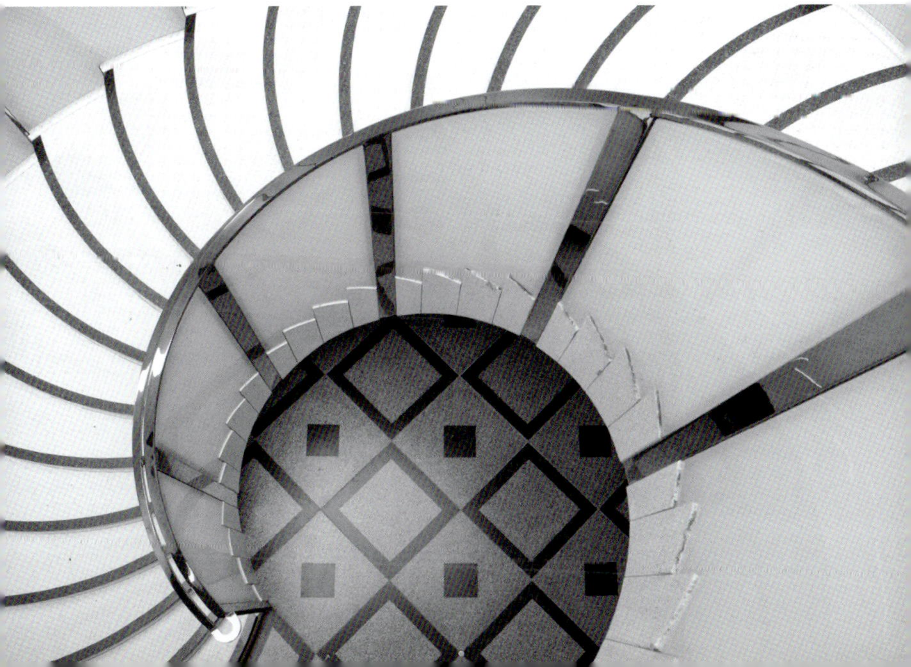

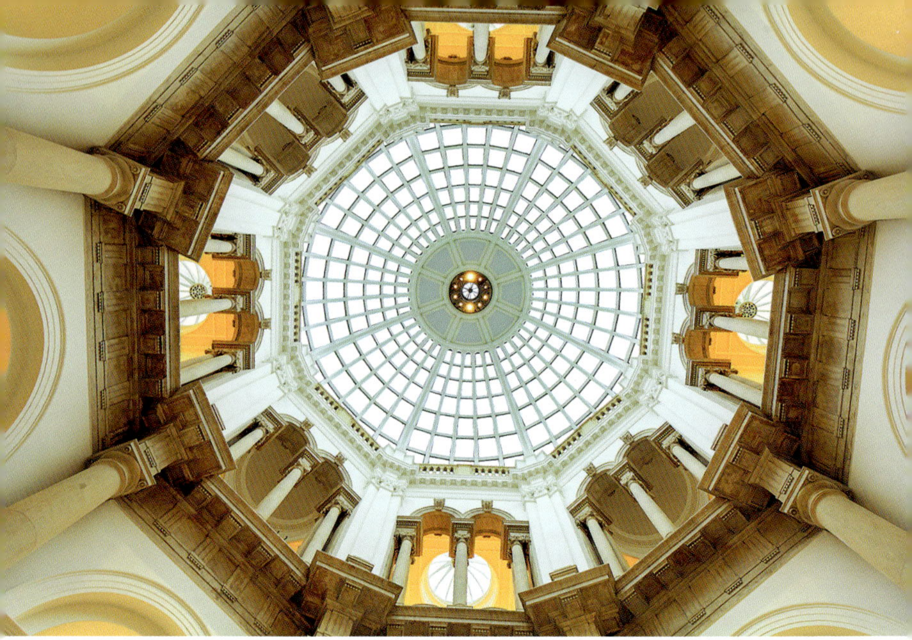

straight up (pictured above), but also try from the inside of the spiral at the foot of the stairs.

Also on the main floor is a long gallery with tall columns and a polished floor that creates some subtle reflections. This huge open space is best captured with people in the shot as they highlight the scale really well.

Finally, there's a very colourful staircase near the Manton Foyer worth investigating too (pictured on the right).

» Practical Information

Tube: Pimlico

Pier: Millbank (boats also run from the Tate Modern to this pier)

Bus: 2, 3, 6, 87, 88, C10

Web: www.tate.org.uk

Tel: 020 7887 8888

Open: 10am – 6pm every day

Closed: 24–26th December

Admission: Free

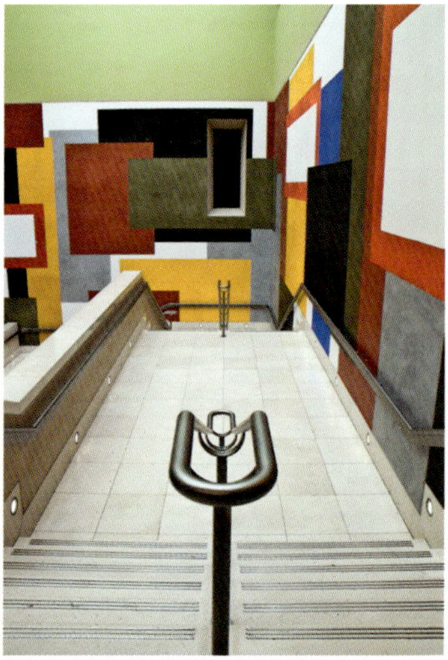

6 WESTMINSTER ABBEY

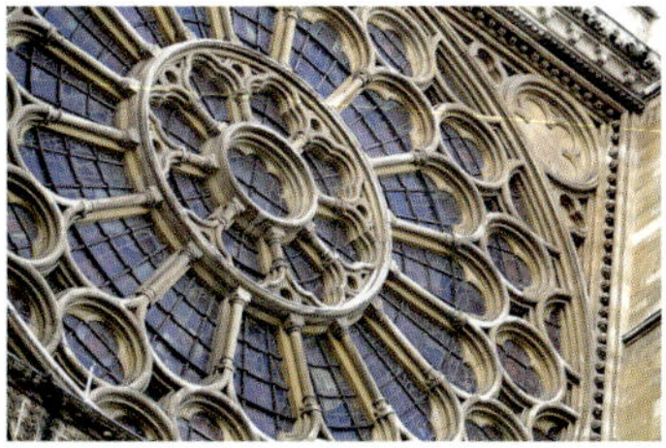

The interior of the abbey is quite magnificent, but unfortunately photography isn't allowed inside (apart from in the cloisters, that is). Luckily, the gothic exterior is fabulous and provides plenty to photograph. The most impressive side is the North Transept (pictured below). The facade is architecturally extravagant, with pointed arches, pinnacles and flying buttresses. It works well photographed straight on and is a good location during the day as well as at night. There are also plenty of subjects to do close-up detail shots of here, such as the ironwork on the doors, the delicate rose window (pictured above) or the stone carvings that adorn the building. The West Front is also very attractive, with two huge towers at the top and yet more detail to do close-ups of. Finally, it's worth visiting the cloisters, which you can do for free without having to pay the entrance charge for the abbey. Here you'll find atmospheric walkways with old flagged floors, vaulted ceilings and decorative arched windows.

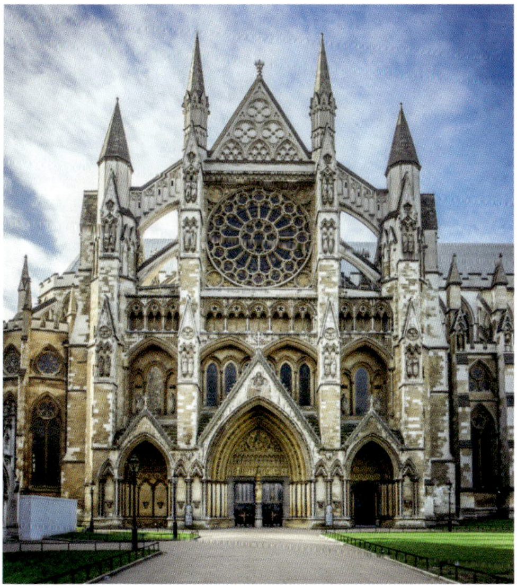

» Practical Information

Tube: Westminster

Pier: Westminster

Bus: 11, 24, 88, 148

Cloisters: Opening times for free entry are the same times as the abbey (see www.westminster-abbey.org as they vary through the year). Use the Cloister Entrance (see page 14 for the location) and make yourself know to a marshal, who will give you an entry card.

7 BUCKINGHAM PALACE

Unsurprisingly, the palace is usually pretty busy during the day, so if you want to photograph the building itself I'd recommend going early in the morning or at night when there are far fewer people around. There are quite a few different viewpoints to explore. The first is from the Victoria Memorial, where you get a head-on view of the palace that includes the grand front gates too. You can also use the fountain surrounding the memorial as foreground, which looks particularly good if you can capture some reflections in it. The second viewpoint is from the gardens behind the memorial, looking across to the palace with the flowers and shrubs as foreground. The third viewpoint is from the middle of the pedestrian crossing at the end of The Mall, with the memorial in the centre of the shot and the palace behind (pictured below). Shooting from further down The Mall also works well, as the trees on either side nicely frame the palace. These views look great with light trails from passing traffic in. There are also various subjects to do detail shots of, such as the guards stationed in their boxes inside the palace courtyard and the extravagant golden crests on the palace gates.

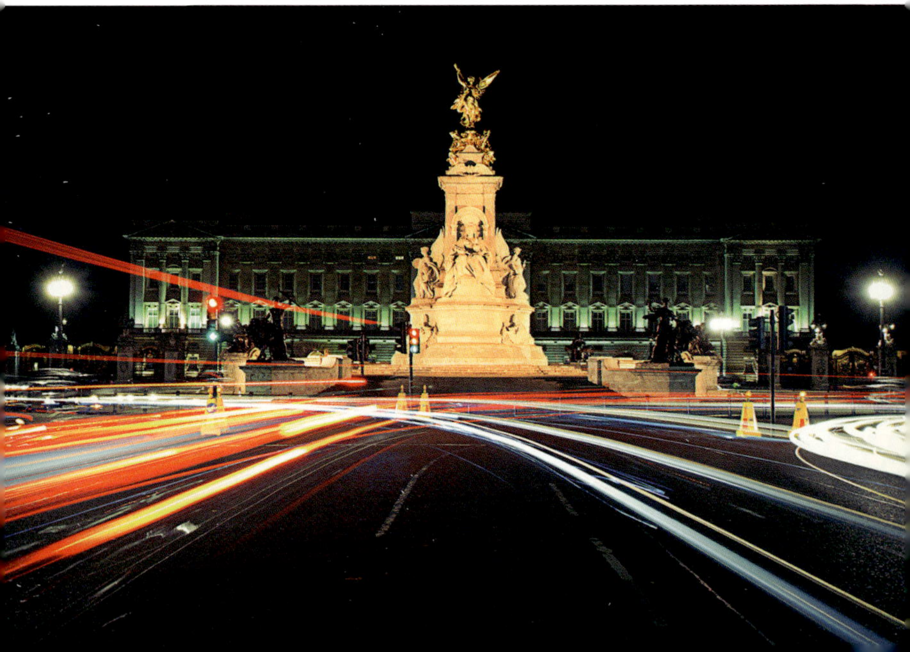

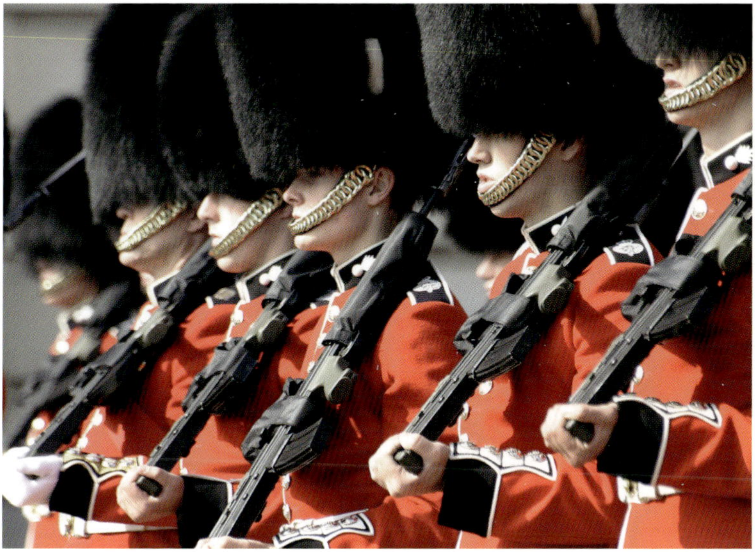

If you want to photograph the Changing of the Guard ceremony (pictured above) be prepared for the crowds as it can get extremely busy. The ceremony takes place inside the palace courtyard, so the best spot to be is right beside the railings on either side of the main gate. From here you can shoot the ceremony through the railings, although you won't be able to see the guards march in as the crowd will build up behind you. If you're visiting in the height of summer I'd recommend going an hour before it starts to claim your spot (in winter you'll probably be safe enough going 30 minutes before). The next best location to capture it from is the steps of the Victoria Memorial. From here you'll get a good view as the guards arrive and will be able to watch the ceremony too, although chances of getting a good photograph of it from here are slim due to the railings. If you don't like crowds then station yourself on either The Mall or Spur Road, where you can catch the guards as they march between their barracks and the palace.

» Practical Information

Tube: St James's Park, Green Park, Victoria, Hyde Park Corner

Bus: 11, 211, C1, C10

Ceremony times: The Changing of the Guard is at 11.30am every day May – July, and on alternate days August – April (see www.changing-guard.com for dates from August to April).

8 ST JAMES'S PARK

St James's Park is the oldest of the Royal Parks in the capital and lies between Whitehall and Buckingham Palace. It's small but beautiful with a charming lake, scattered trees and winding paths. One of the best locations for photography in the park is Blue Bridge, which crosses the lake roughly in the middle. From here there's an attractive view east over the lake towards Horse Guards and Whitehall, with the London Eye peeking out over the top of the buildings (pictured below). Looking west from the bridge you'll get a view over the water to Buckingham Palace, framed on either side by trees. Both of these views are best with low wind (to get good reflections) and a blue sky. It's also worth investigating the avenue of trees on the north side of the park, as well as the lakeside path (especially around the fountains at the eastern end), to see what other views you can find. On top of that, there's plenty of wildlife to photograph in the park, from ducks and geese to incredibly tame grey squirrels and even a resident colony of pelicans. The park is at its best from spring, when you'll find daffodils and cherry trees in blossom, through to autumn when the trees turn golden.

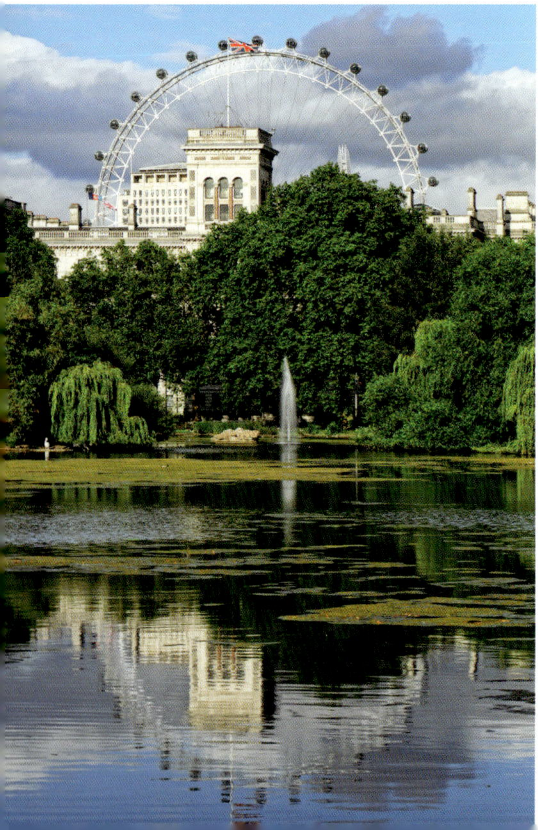

» Practical Information

Tube: St James's Park, Charing Cross, Green Park, Westminster

Bus: 3, 9, 11, 24, 148, 159, 211, 453

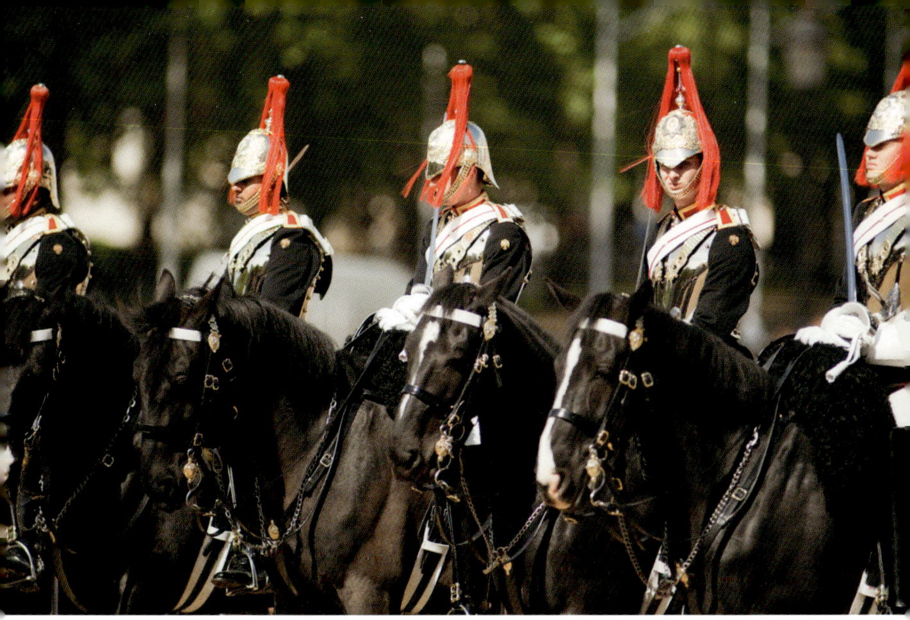

9 HORSE GUARDS PARADE

Horse Guards Parade is a large parade ground found between St James's Park and Whitehall. Every morning a ceremony is held here where two sets of mounted guards change over. The ceremony lasts around half an hour, giving you plenty of time to photograph the horses and guards in their ceremonial uniform. It's usually much quieter than the Changing of the Guard at Buckingham Palace and there are no railings in the way, so it's a lot easier to photograph (the only tricky bit is trying to block out the other people watching).

The horses approach from The Mall, so if you can't find a good spot in the parade ground you can always try to capture them as they arrive. After the ceremony ends you'll find mounted sentries on the Whitehall side of the building all day until 4pm, when a smaller and shorter dismounting ceremony is held in the courtyard of the Horse Guards building.

» Practical Information

Tube: Charing Cross, Embankment

Bus: 11, 24, 88, 159, 453

Ceremony times: The Changing of the Guard is at 11am Monday to Saturday and 10am on Sundays. The dismounting ceremony is at 4pm every day.

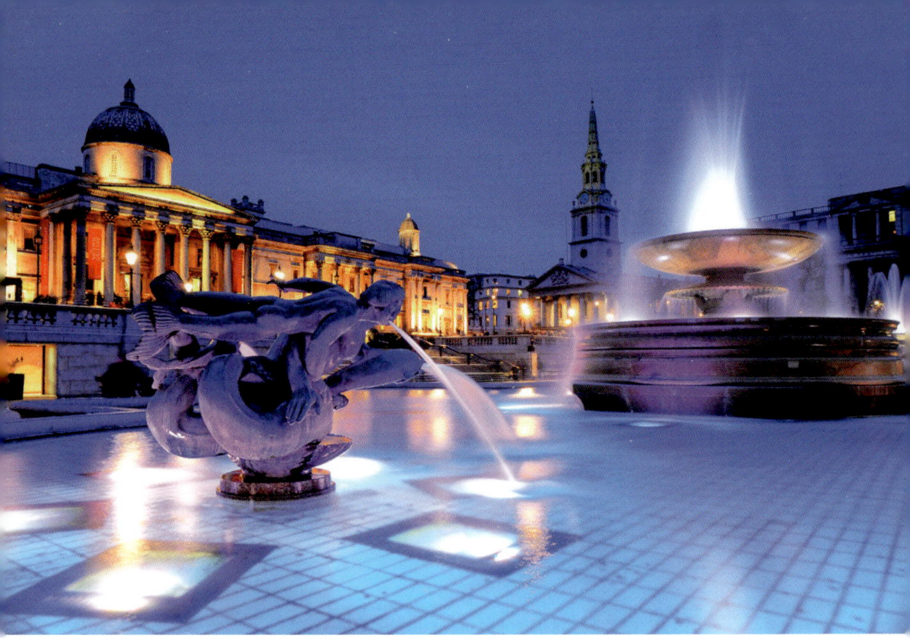

10 TRAFALGAR SQUARE

The most popular subjects to photograph in this huge square are the National Gallery and Nelson's Column, which is guarded at the base by four giant bronze lion statues.

To capture the National Gallery try standing in the middle of the square between the two fountains. This gives you a symmetrical view of the facade with the steps leading your eye up to the grand front entrance. The fountains can also be used to great effect as interesting foreground, especially if you can include some reflections in the water. The western fountain is best for this as the view incorporates the spire of St Martin in the Fields Church as well (pictured above). The steps and railings in front of the National Gallery also make equally good foreground (pictured bottom right). The compositions are generally more photogenic after rain as you get subtle reflections in the paving.

To take in the whole of the square a good location is the terrace in front of the National Gallery. The added height of the terrace gives you a better perspective and you can just about get the top of Nelson's Column in too. The column is very tall, so if you want to capture it in detail it's best to get a bit closer and shoot at an angle looking up at it. It looks best set against a blue sky, but including a nearby statue in the frame also helps add interest.

Another great subject to photograph are the lions. A composition that works really well is to juxtapose them against the surrounding buildings, for example the National Gallery or Big Ben (pictured on the right).

The square gets very busy during the day (even at quiet times of the year), so I'd recommend going very early in the morning or at night when there are fewer people milling around. Saying that, during the day it's a great place to do candid street photography, as most people are so busy taking their own photos or having a rest from sightseeing that you won't be noticed.

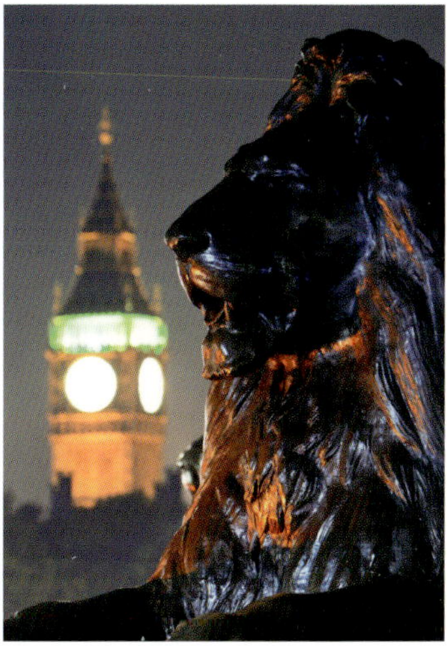

» Practical Information

Tube: Charing Cross, Embankment

Pier: Embankment

Bus: 9, 11, 13, 15, 23, 24, 139, 159, 453

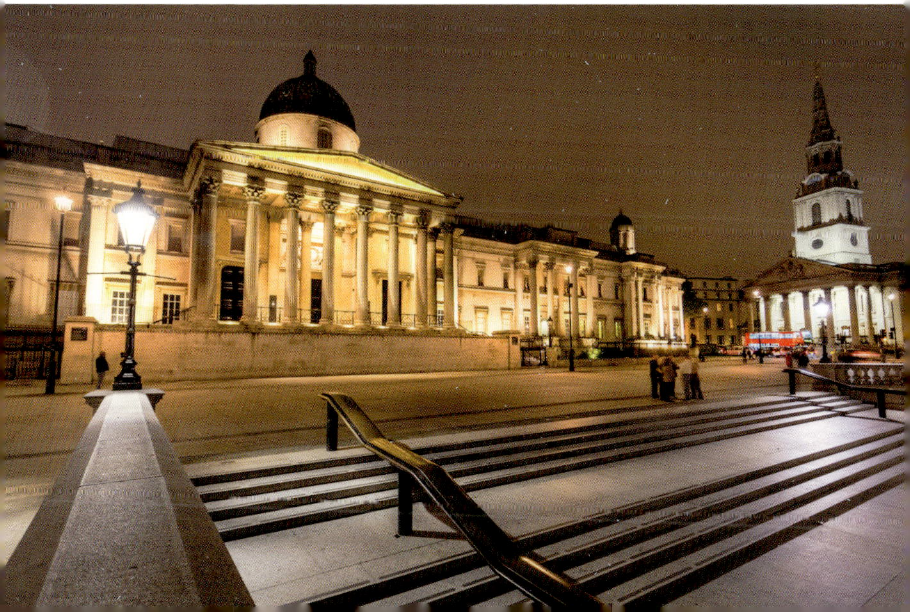

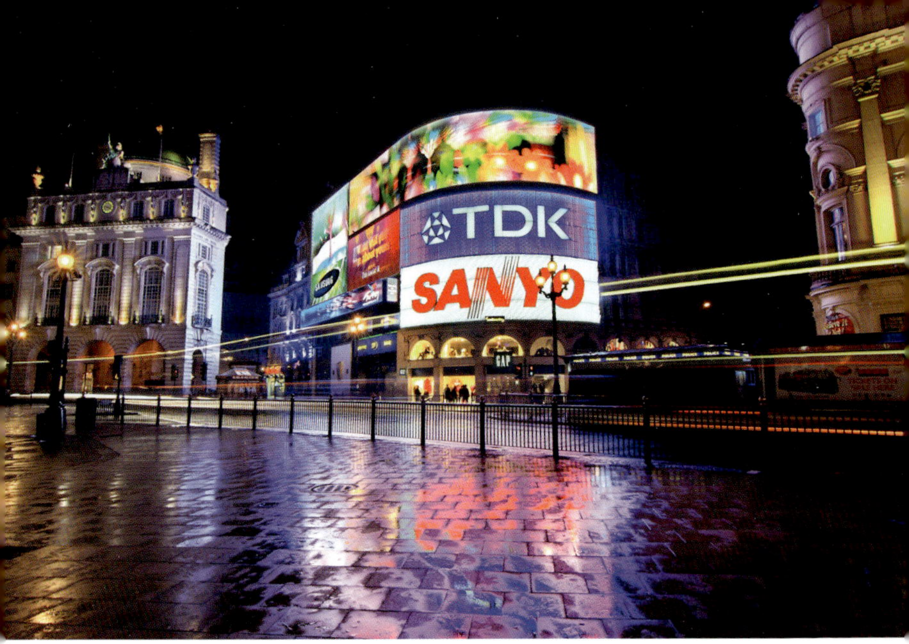

11 PICCADILLY CIRCUS

Piccadilly Circus is a busy intersection in the West End that's always bustling with people, even at night. It's famous for the iconic Statue of Eros and the neon advertising signs that adorn the buildings on the northern side (pictured above). The best time to photograph it is at night, as the neon signs are more prominent and there are endless opportunities to include light trails from passing traffic in your composition. The statue is best captured during the day isolated against a blue sky, but if you're there at night try silhouetting it against the neon signs instead. It's much more photogenic after a little bit of rain, as the reflections add an extra dimension to the scene. There isn't a classic composition here, so make sure you explore all the way around the junction to see what you can find (the statue and the underground signs make particularly good foreground elements). It's also worth checking out the view from Piccadilly Circus looking along the elegant curve of Regent Street.

» Practical Information

Tube: Piccadilly Circus

Bus: 13, 14, 15, 23, 38, 139, 159, 453

12 CHINA TOWN

Since the 1950s the area around Gerrard Street in Soho has been the centre of London's Chinese community. It's packed with Chinese restaurants and shops, and is best captured at night when the streets are most colourful. Two particularly good spots for capturing street scenes are at either end of Gerrard Street, where there are tall Chinese gates you can include in your composition. Also, the shop and restaurant windows make for interesting close-up photos (look out for succulent roast ducks in restaurant windows, cakes in bakery windows and unusual packaging or displays in shops and supermarkets). The best time of year to visit is at Chinese New Year, which falls somewhere between late January and mid February. Although it's busy during this period the streets are decorated with hundreds of lanterns, adding even more interest and atmosphere (pictured below).

» Practical Information

Tube: Leicester Square, Piccadilly Circus

Bus: 14, 19, 24, 29, 38, 176

Web: www.chinatownlondon.org

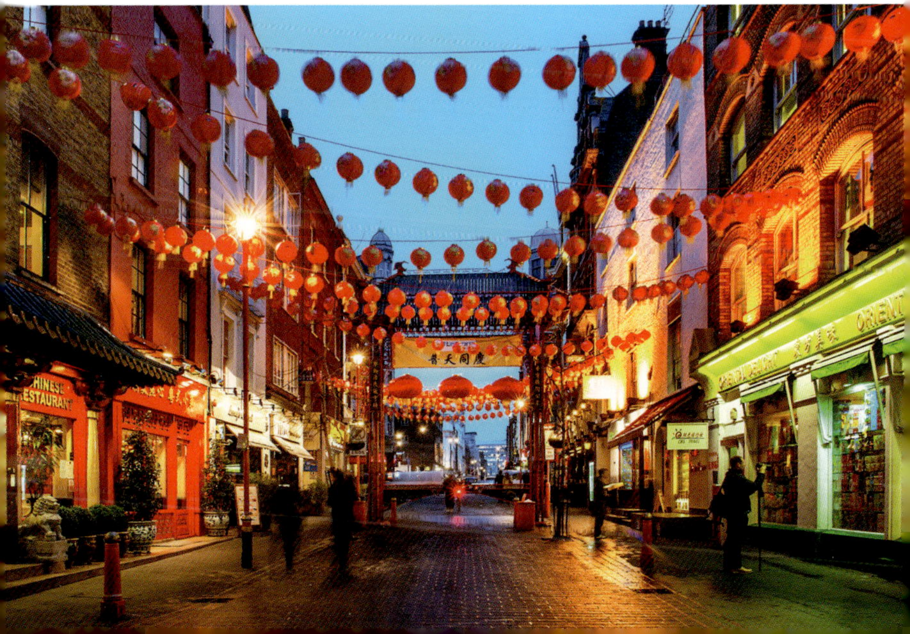

13 COVENT GARDEN

At the heart of the Covent Garden district you'll find the Central Market. The market is packed with shops and stalls selling things like souvenirs, arts and crafts, and is surrounded by an open–air cobbled piazza. It's a very popular tourist destination, but also a great place for street photography. The biggest draw are the street–performers that entertain the crowds all around the piazza (pictured below). They range from jugglers to living statues and pretty much everything in between. Also, just a two minute walk from here is one of the best places in London to photograph the iconic red phone box. Head

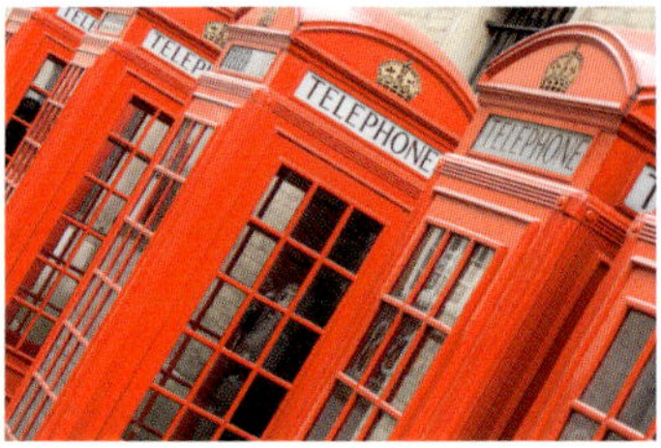

for the corner of the Royal Opera House, where Bow Street meets Broad Court, and you'll find five of them in a row (pictured above). There's also an elegant ballerina statue here, which is interesting to shoot with the phone boxes as background. (It makes good foreground for night photos of the Royal Opera House too.)

» Practical Information

Tube: Covent Garden, Leicester Square

Bus: RV1

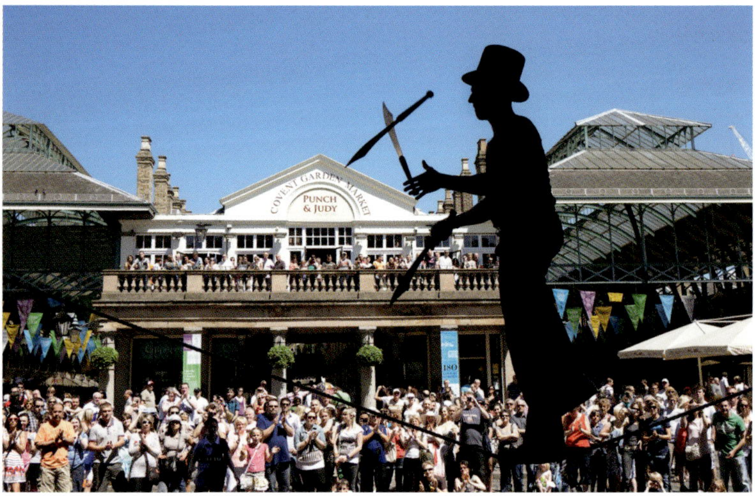

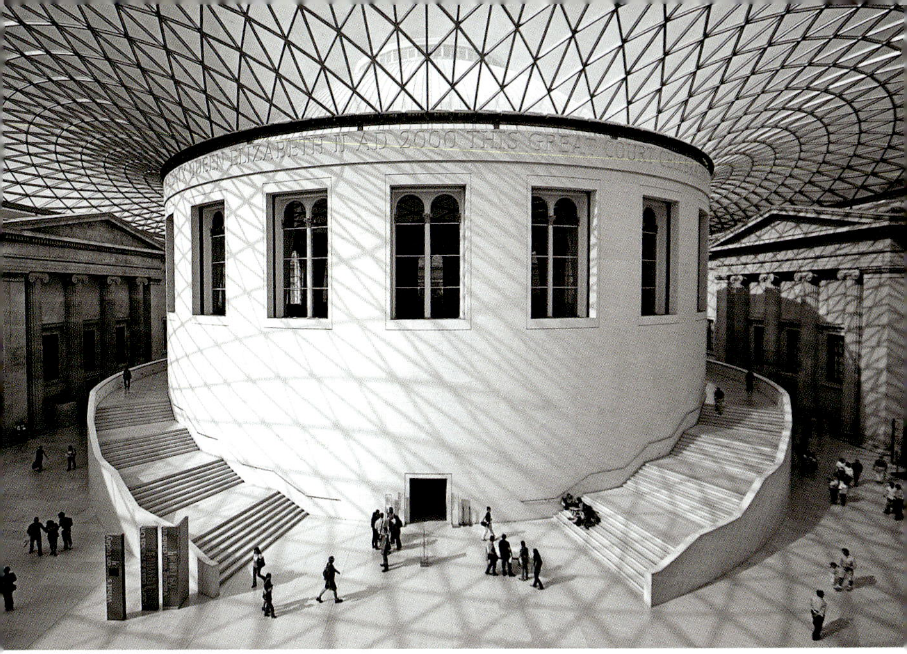

14 THE BRITISH MUSEUM

The main subject of photographic interest in this huge museum is the Great Court, which has a stunning steel and glass roof. On Level 3, above the main entrance, you'll find a good vantage point to take it all in (pictured above). Abstract shots isolating sections of the building along with the roof also work really well. An interesting feature to focus on are the stairs that wind around the central reading room – try shooting them from Level 3 (perhaps with a person in for scale), the foot of the stairs and the top of the stairs. It's best visited on a sunny day as the roof casts patterned shadows that really add to the scene. The grand neo-classical front entrance on Great Russell Street is also photogenic, especially at night when the columns are lit up.

» Practical Information

Tube: Tottenham Court Road, Holborn

Bus: 8, 24, 25, 29, 38, 98, 188, 390

Web: www.britishmuseum.org

Tel: 020 7323 8299

Open: 9am – 6pm (8.30pm on Fridays)

Closed: 1st January, 24–26th December

Admission: Free

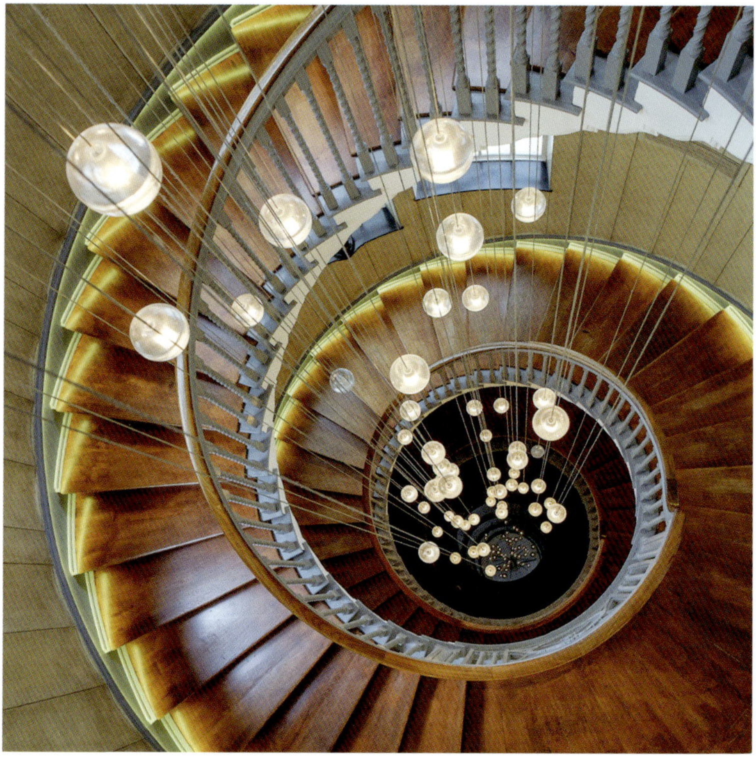

15 THE BREWER STAIRCASE

This striking spiral staircase is nestled at the back of the historic Heal's store on Tottenham Court Road. It was designed and built in 1916 by Cecil Brewer and Heal's are very friendly towards photographers who want to capture it. Its graceful curves are immensely photogenic and an elegant chandelier of glass baubles hangs down through the spiral, adding even more interest to the scene. The staircase is equally good shot looking up as it is looking down, so make sure you investigate both views (and do so from different floors too). Also, try standing right at the foot of the stairs looking straight up through the spiral.

» Practical Information

Tube: Goodge Street

Bus: 10, 14, 24, 29, 73, 134, 390

Open: 10am – 7pm Monday to Saturday, 12 noon – 6pm Sunday

3 SECTION North London

One of the main areas of interest on the northern side of central London is Camden Town (often shortened to just 'Camden'). It's famous for its complex of markets, which are fun to explore and great for street photography, although they can get extremely busy at weekends. It also has a colourful high street with some elaborately decorated buildings, and the area around Camden Lock is very picturesque in the summer. If you're interested in canal scenery Regent's Canal runs right through the heart of Camden. (Although if you like photographing this sort of scenery a better location is Little Venice, which is to the southwest near Paddington Station and can be reached by boat trip from Camden.)

A short walk from Camden is Primrose Hill, which is a small hill with good views to central London. To the south of here is Regent's Park – the largest of the Royal Parks in central London. The northeastern corner is home to London Zoo, which is one of the best in the world and so an obvious choice if you want to squeeze some wildlife photography into your visit. There are also some lovely formal gardens in the park too (see page 104 for more).

There are a couple of notable tube and train stations in the north – Baker Street Tube Station and King's Cross Train Station. Baker Street is one of the oldest stations in London and has some characterful platforms, whereas the main concourse at King's Cross has a modern new roof that's extremely photogenic. If you're at King's Cross and enjoy gothic architecture then I'd recommend also paying a visit to the St Pancras Renaissance Hotel next door.

If you're after more locations in the northern area then I'd recommend Highgate Cemetery, which is an unusual but rewarding location to photograph (see page 102 for more), and the metal spiral staircase at the Wellcome Collection museum on Euston Road.

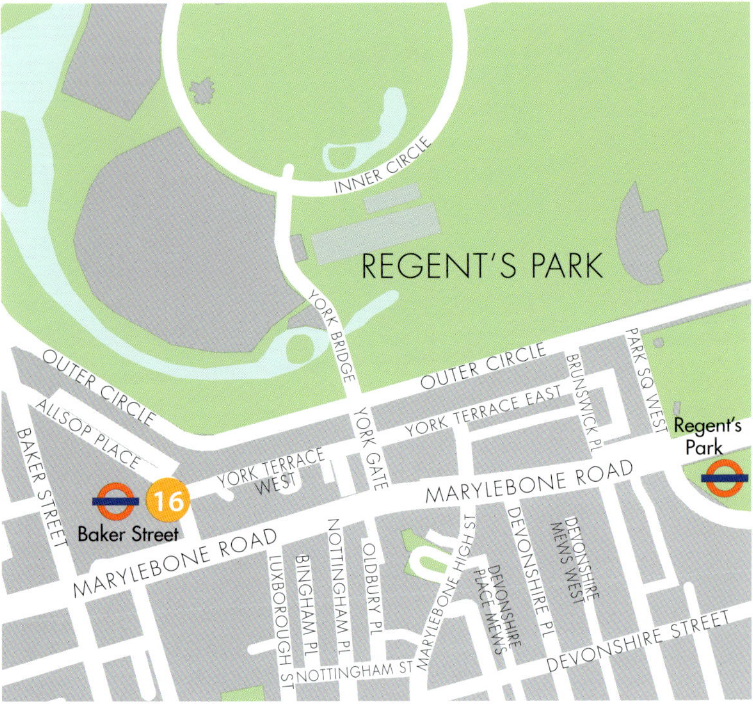
REGENT'S PARK
INNER CIRCLE
YORK BRIDGE
OUTER CIRCLE
OUTER CIRCLE
ALLSOP PLACE
BAKER STREET
YORK TERRACE WEST
YORK GATE
YORK TERRACE EAST
BRUNSWICK PL
PARK SQ WEST
Regent's Park
16
Baker Street
MARYLEBONE ROAD
MARYLEBONE ROAD
LUXBOROUGH ST
BINGHAM PL
NOTTINGHAM PL
OLDBURY PL
MARYLEBONE HIGH ST
DEVONSHIRE PLACE MEWS
DEVONSHIRE PL
DEVONSHIRE MEWS WEST
DEVONSHIRE STREET
NOTTINGHAM ST

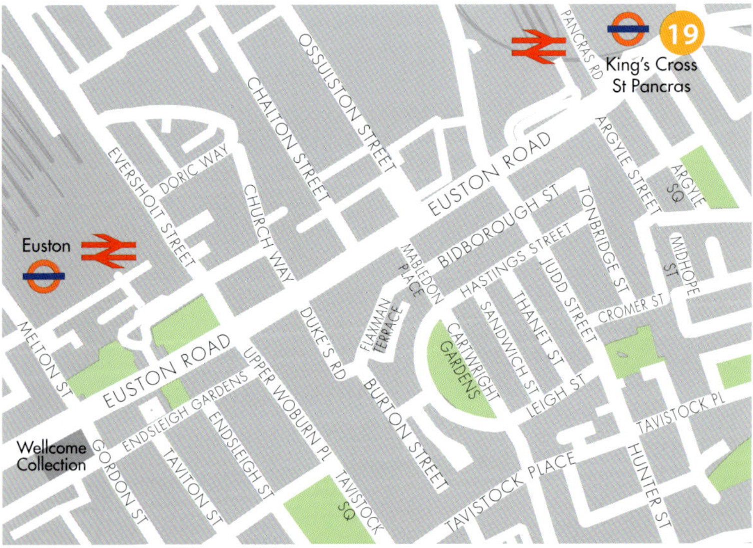
PANCRAS RD
19
King's Cross St Pancras
OSSULSTON STREET
CHALTON STREET
EVERSHOLT STREET
DORIC WAY
CHURCH WAY
EUSTON ROAD
ARGYLE STREET
ARGYLE SQ
BIDBOROUGH ST
TONBRIDGE ST
Euston
MABLEDON PLACE
HASTINGS STREET
JUDD STREET
MIDHOPE ST
CROMER ST
FLAXMAN TERRACE
CARTWRIGHT GARDENS
SANDWICH ST
THANET ST
DUKE'S RD
MELTON ST
EUSTON ROAD
UPPER WOBURN PL
ENDSLEIGH GARDENS
BURTON STREET
LEIGH ST
TAVISTOCK PL
Wellcome Collection
GORDON ST
ENDSLEIGH PL
TAVITON ST
ENDSLEIGH ST
TAVISTOCK SQ
TAVISTOCK PLACE
HUNTER ST

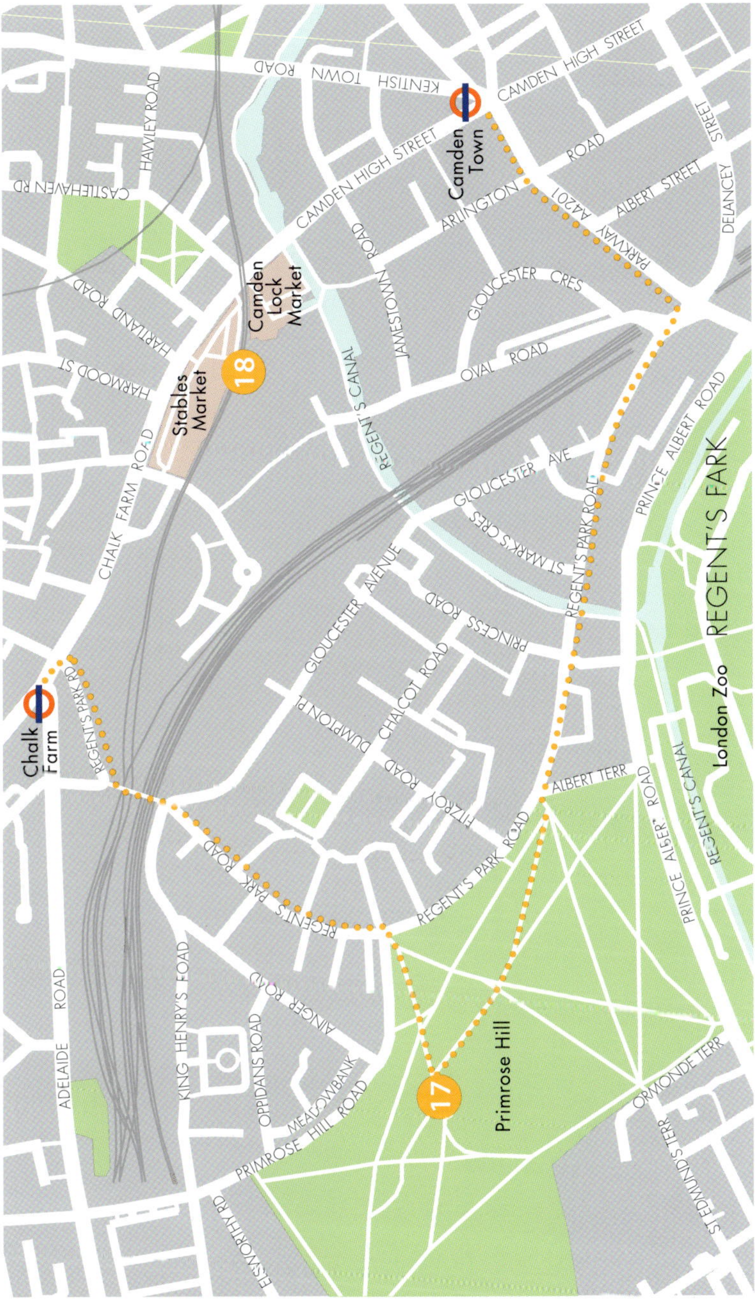
Chalk Farm
Camden Town
Camden Lock Market
Stables Market
18
17
Primrose Hill
REGENT'S PARK
London Zoo
KENTISH TOWN ROAD
CAMDEN HIGH STREET
CASTLEHAVEN RD
HAWLEY ROAD
HARTLAND ROAD
HARMOOD ST
CHALK FARM ROAD
REGENT'S CANAL
JAMESTOWN ROAD
ARLINGTON ROAD
PARKWAY A4201
ALBERT STREET
DELANCEY STREET
GLOUCESTER CRES
OVAL ROAD
GLOUCESTER AVE
ST MARK'S CRES
REGENT'S PARK ROAD
REGENT'S PARK RD
PRINCE ALBERT ROAD
GLOUCESTER AVENUE
PRINCESS ROAD
CHALCOT ROAD
DUMPTON PL
FITZROY ROAD
ALBERT TERR
ADELAIDE ROAD
KING HENRY'S ROAD
OPPIDANS ROAD
AINGER ROAD
MEADOWBANK
PRIMROSE HILL ROAD
ELSWORTHY RD
ORMONDE TERR
ST EDMUND'S TERR

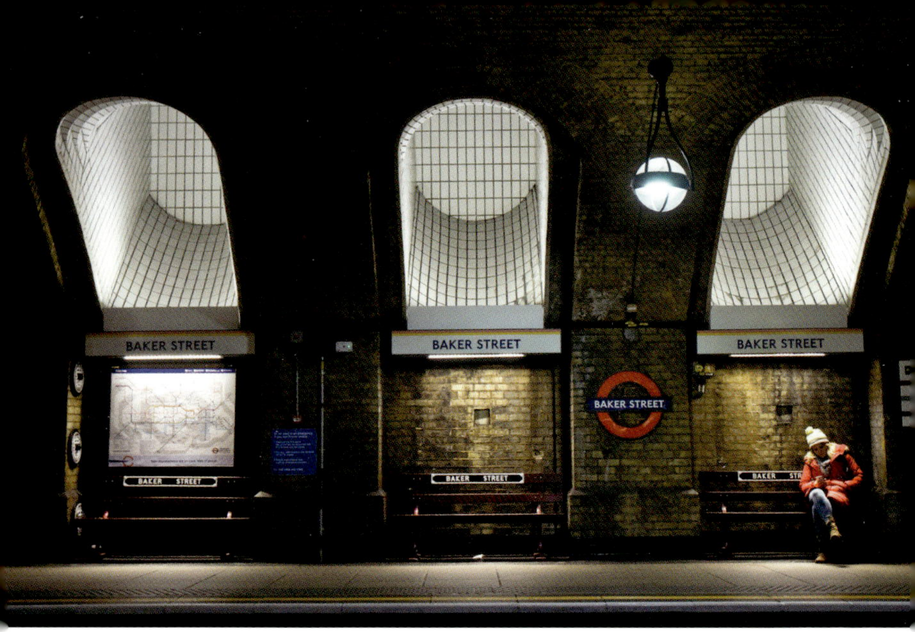

16 BAKER STREET TUBE STATION

This tube station is one of the oldest on the underground network and although it has changed substantially over the years parts of the original station have been well preserved. The best platforms to visit are 5 and 6 (for the Hammersmith & City and Circle lines), which date back to 1863. These platforms are packed full of character, with exposed brickwork, tiled downlit coves and old-fashioned wooden waiting benches (pictured above). The two platforms face each other, so you can stand on one and shoot across the tracks to the other (N.B. it's usually quite dark but tripods and flash aren't allowed). Also, the more modern Bakerloo line platforms are worth a visit while you're there for the Sherlock Holmes wall motifs (pictured below).

» Practical Information

Once in the station just follow the signs for the Hammersmith & City and Circle lines. See page 105 for important info about taking photos in tube stations. Unfortunately, the platforms of interest aren't currently wheelchair accessible.

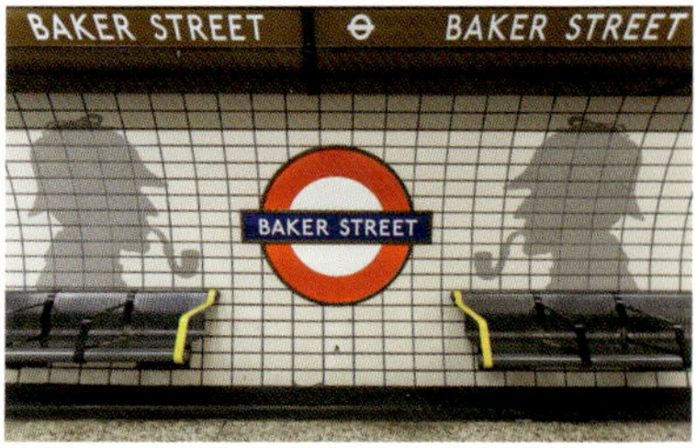

17 PRIMROSE HILL

Just to the north of Regent's Park and London Zoo you'll find Primrose Hill. At only 64 metres it's not the highest hill in the world, but it does have a clear view southeast to central London. From the top you can see various landmarks peeking over the treetops, such as the Shard, the London Eye and the dome of St Paul's. There is some foreground in the form of scattered trees and lampposts, but you'll need an interesting sky or good light to get a great shot here (panoramic format works particularly well). It's best at sunrise but is also really good at night (pictured below). Do be aware that it's over three miles from the Thames, so you'll need to zoom in a fair bit to fill the frame.

» Practical Information

Tube: Chalk Farm or Camden Town. Chalk Farm is closest, but it's about 15 minutes from either station (routes are shown on the map on page 34). For a slightly longer but more pleasant walk, follow the canal path west from Camden Lock and turn north when you reach Regent's Park.

Bus: 274, C2

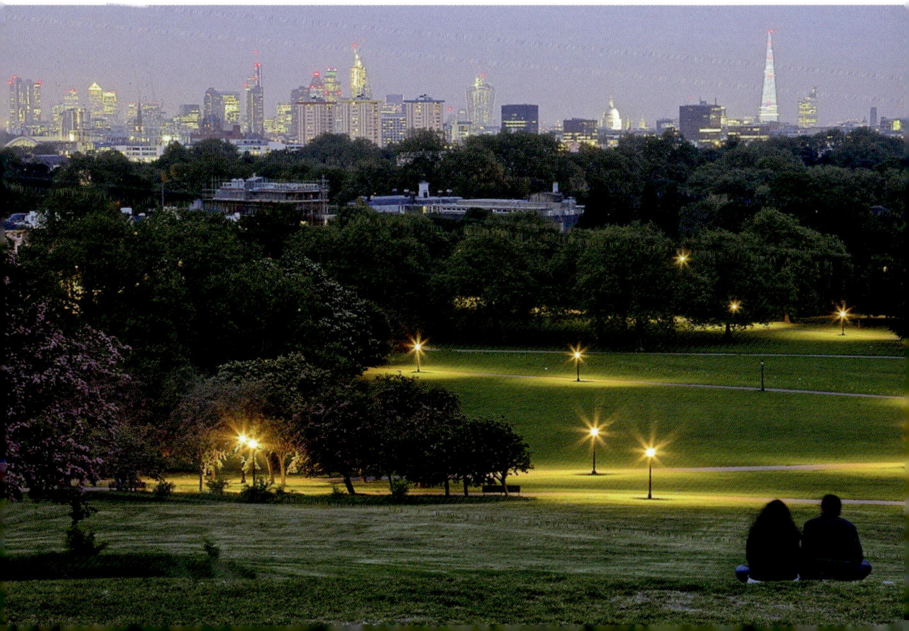

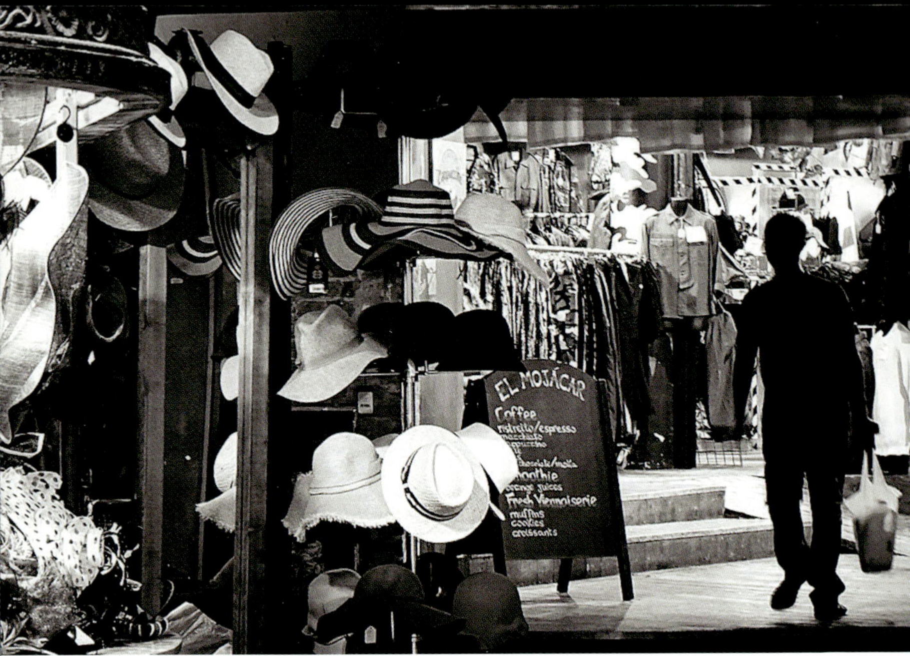

18 CAMDEN MARKET

Camden Market is actually a collection of a few different markets along Camden High Street – the Electric Ballroom, Camden Market, Inverness Street Market, Camden Lock Market and the Stables Market. The most interesting photographically are Camden Lock Market and the Stables Market (pictured above). Wandering through the various buildings, cobbled streets and alleyways you'll find an eclectic mix of shops and stalls selling things like art, crafts, clothing and jewellery. There's plenty of attractive and unusual displays to photograph and it's also a really good place for street photography as the area is a magnet for the young alternative crowd. The markets are a bit of a labyrinth, so it's not uncommon to get lost, but that's part of the fun of exploring them. There's always something open every day of the week, but it's best to visit from Thursday to Sunday when the majority of stalls are open. It can get very busy at weekends, so if you're not a fan of crowds I'd recommend going on a Thursday or Friday.

» Practical Information

Tube: Camden Town, Chalk Farm
Bus: 24, 27, 168, 274, C2
Open: 10am – 6pm every day

19 KING'S CROSS STATION

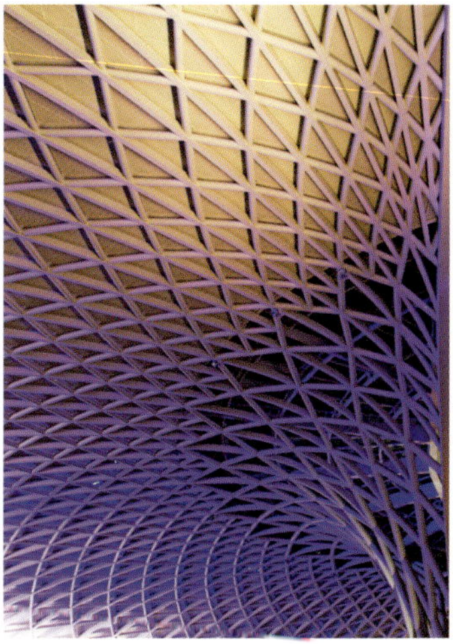

The star attraction at King's Cross Train Station is the stunning metal roof in the main concourse, which emerges from the floor and spreads into a lattice overhead. It's fascinating to photograph and there are plenty of different compositions to explore. For example, if you stand at the base of the structure and look straight up you get an unusual but striking view (pictured below). For another unusual view, try standing behind the base of the structure and looking up. Abstract shots of the gridwork that completely fill the frame also work really well (pictured above).

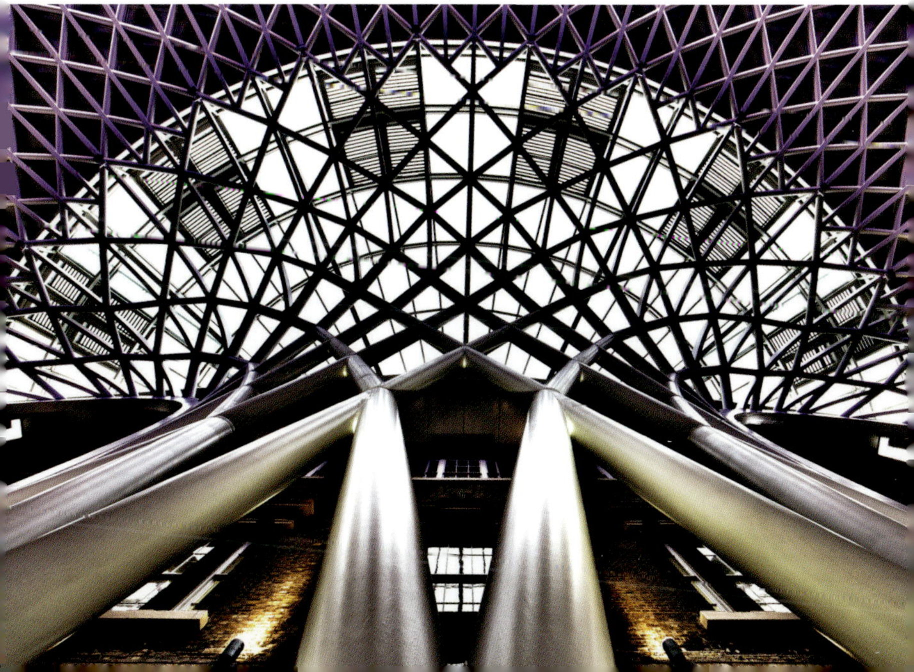

To take in the wider scene the upper mezzanine level provides an excellent vantage point. If you stand in the middle, opposite where the metalwork emerges from the floor, you get a really good symmetrical view of the lattice fanning out, set against the brick building behind. Or try from either end of the mezzanine, using the curved balcony railings as foreground. The location is equally good during the day as it is at night, but be aware that tripods and flash photography aren't allowed in the station.

While at King's Cross, make sure you also visit the light tunnel beneath the station (pictured below). This curved tunnel has a backlit wall along one side that constantly cycles through various soft pastel colours. Including a lone person in the scene adds scale and interest, particularly if you can include their reflection in the light wall as well.

» Practical Information

King's Cross is accessible by many tube, train and bus routes. To find the light tunnel, go down one level into the underground station and follow the signs for St Pancras. You'll find the tunnel, which leads to Pancras Square, on your right–hand side. See page 105 for important information about taking photos in tube or train stations.

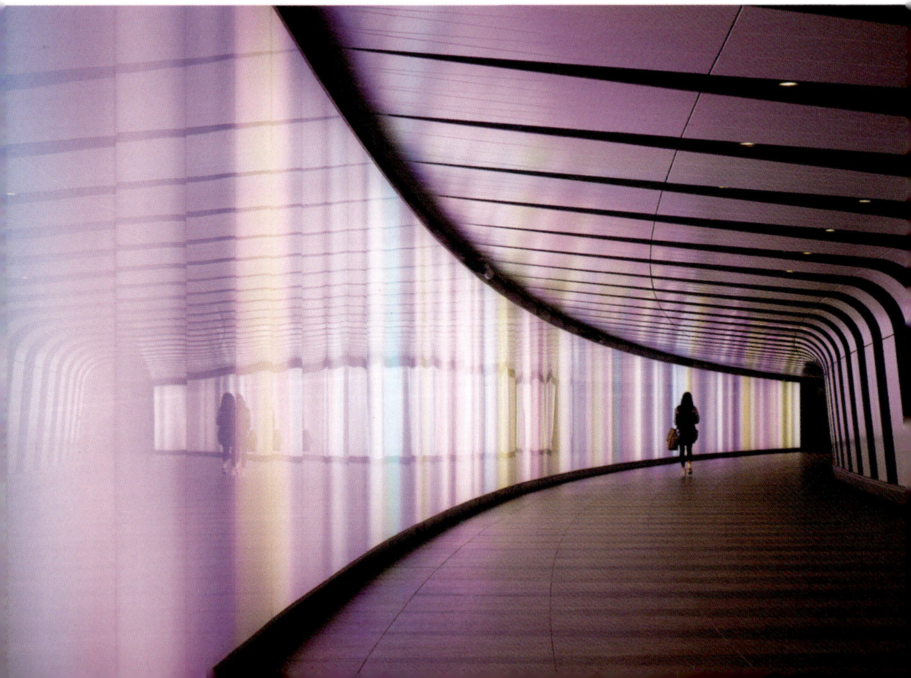

4 SECTION South Bank, Bankside & Southwark

The southern bank of the Thames between Westminster Bridge and Tower Bridge is packed with photographic opportunities. The area between Westminster Bridge and Blackfriars Bridge, known as the South Bank, is home to the iconic London Eye and is also the best place from which to capture The Houses of Parliament and Big Ben. There are plenty of bridges that offer great views too, such as Waterloo Bridge and the pedestrian bridges that flank the Hungerford Bridge (which are called the Golden Jubilee Bridges). In this area there are also a couple of great locations for photographing graffiti – Leake Street and Southbank Skate Park. The area is most photogenic at night, but it's great during the day for street photography as people meander along the waterfront.

Moving east from Blackfriars Bridge you come to the Bankside area. The main photographic attraction in this area is the Millennium Bridge, which is a favourite location with many people. It is heavily photographed, but for good reason as it's so picturesque and has an interesting background. There's also the Tate Modern art gallery, which has a stark modern interior that's great for candid people shots.

Beside London Bridge you'll find Southwark Cathedral – one of the most beautiful places of worship in London, and right next door is an interesting food market called Borough Market. Towering over London Bridge Station is the Shard, which is the tallest building in the UK and has a purpose built viewing gallery at the top. Although it's not cheap to visit the views are unsurpassed. If you're looking for even more locations in the area, London Bridge itself also makes great foreground for photos of the City (shot from the southern side of the river) or for the Shard (shot from the northern side).

Tower Bridge needs no introduction and there are multiple viewpoints from which to shoot it, but there are also plenty of opportunities at neighbouring City Hall and the More London development. Hay's Galleria is also worth a look for its metal and glass roof.

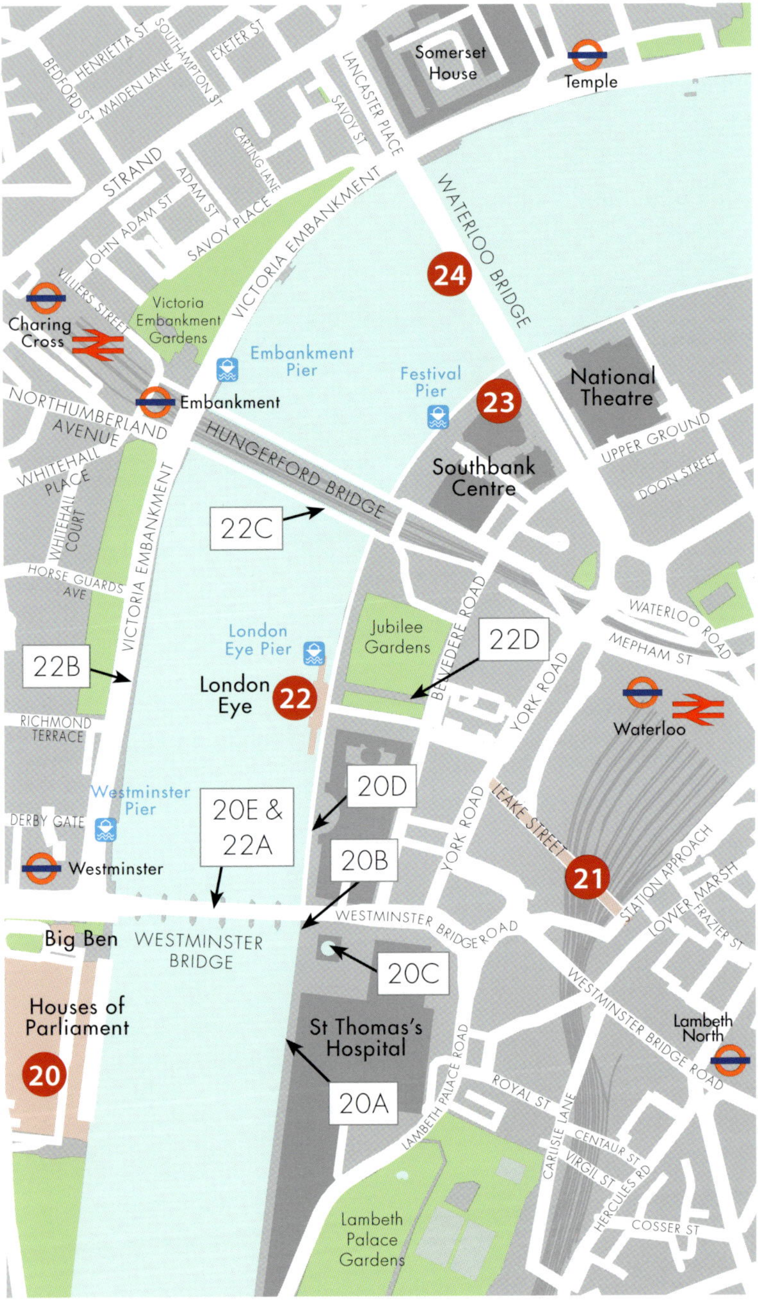
Somerset House
Temple
BEDFORD ST
HENRIETTA ST
MAIDEN LANE
SOUTHAMPTON ST
EXETER ST
LANCASTER PLACE
SAVOY ST
CARTING LANE
STRAND
ADAM ST
JOHN ADAM ST
SAVOY PLACE
VICTORIA EMBANKMENT
WATERLOO BRIDGE
24
Charing Cross
VILLIERS STREET
Victoria Embankment Gardens
Embankment Pier
Festival Pier
23
National Theatre
Embankment
NORTHUMBERLAND AVENUE
HUNGERFORD BRIDGE
Southbank Centre
UPPER GROUND
DOON STREET
WHITEHALL PLACE
WHITEHALL COURT
22C
VICTORIA EMBANKMENT
HORSE GUARDS AVE
BELVEDERE ROAD
WATERLOO ROAD
MEPHAM ST
London Eye Pier
Jubilee Gardens
22D
22B
London Eye
22
YORK ROAD
Waterloo
RICHMOND TERRACE
20D
LEAKE STREET
Westminster Pier
20E & 22A
YORK ROAD
DERBY GATE
20B
21
STATION APPROACH
Westminster
LOWER MARSH
FRAZIER ST
WESTMINSTER BRIDGE ROAD
Big Ben
WESTMINSTER BRIDGE
20C
Houses of Parliament
St Thomas's Hospital
WESTMINSTER BRIDGE ROAD
Lambeth North
20
20A
LAMBETH PALACE ROAD
ROYAL ST
CARLISLE LANE
CENTAUR ST
VIRGIL ST
HERCULES RD
COSSER ST
Lambeth Palace Gardens

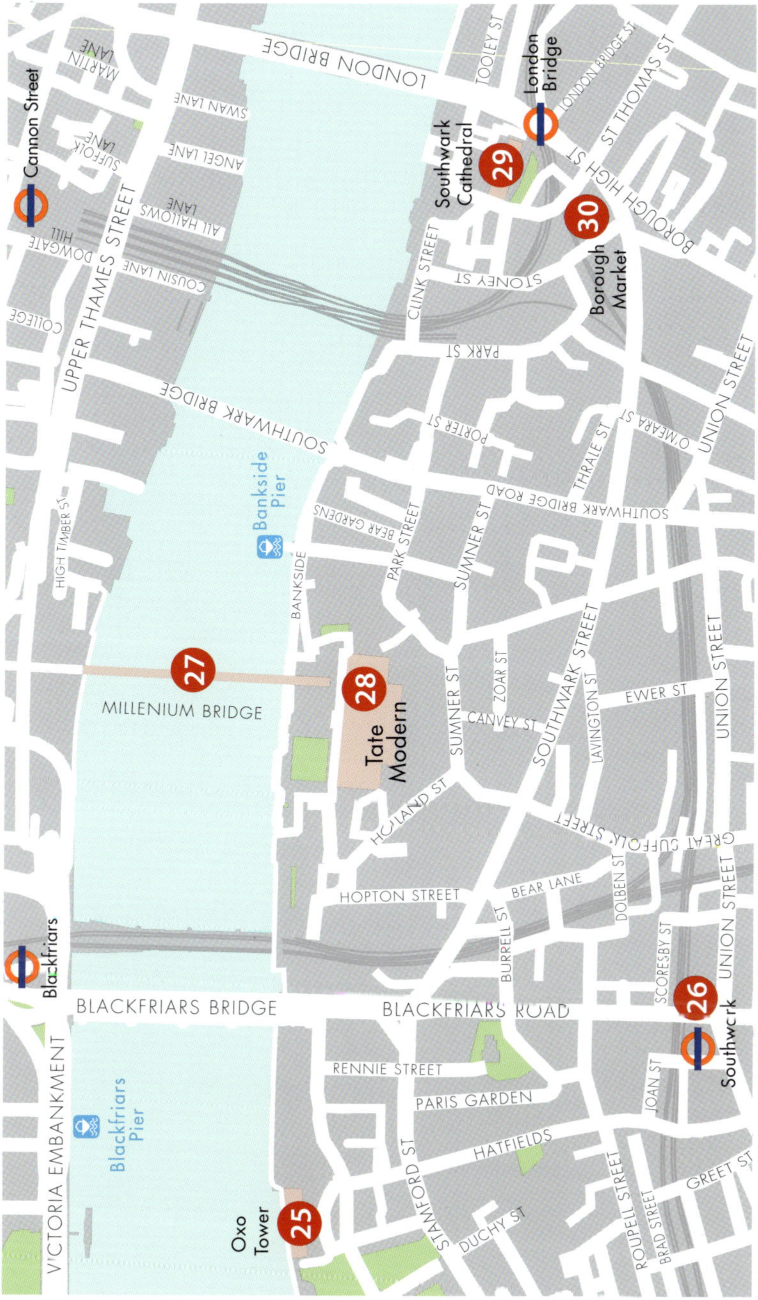
Cannon Street
London Bridge
Southwark Cathedral
Borough Market
Tate Modern
Bankside Pier
Blackfriars
Blackfriars Pier
Oxo Tower
Southwark
25
26
27
28
29
30
LONDON BRIDGE
SOUTHWARK BRIDGE
MILLENIUM BRIDGE
BLACKFRIARS BRIDGE
BLACKFRIARS ROAD
VICTORIA EMBANKMENT
UPPER THAMES STREET
MARTIN LANE
SWAN LANE
ANGEL LANE
SUFFOLK LANE
ALL HALLOWS LANE
DOWGATE HILL
COUSIN LANE
COLLEGE
HIGH TIMBER ST
TOOLEY ST
LONDON BRIDGE ST
ST THOMAS ST
BOROUGH HIGH ST
CLINK STREET
STONEY ST
PARK ST
PORTER ST
O'MEARA ST
THRALE ST
UNION STREET
SOUTHWARK BRIDGE ROAD
BEAR GARDENS
PARK STREET
BANKSIDE
SUMNER ST
ZOAR ST
SOUTHWARK STREET
LAVINGTON ST
EWER ST
CANVEY ST
HOLLAND ST
GREAT SUFFOLK STREET
HOPTON STREET
BEAR LANE
DOLBEN ST
BURRELL ST
SCORESBY ST
RENNIE STREET
PARIS GARDEN
JOAN ST
HATFIELDS
STAMFORD ST
DUCHY ST
ROUPELL STREET
BRAD STREET
GREET ST

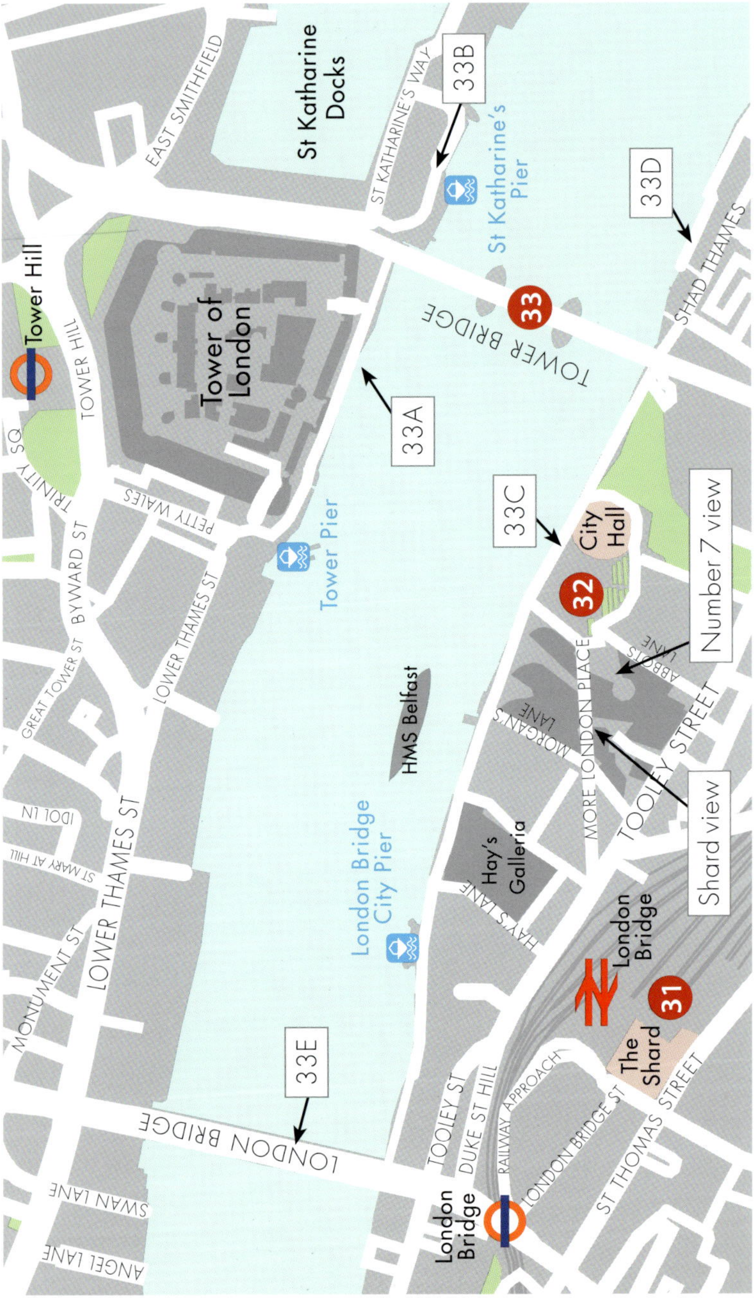
St Katharine Docks
EAST SMITHFIELD
ST KATHARINE'S WAY
33B
St Katharine's Pier
33D
SHAD THAMES
Tower Hill
TOWER HILL
TRINITY SQ
Tower of London
33
TOWER BRIDGE
33A
PETTY WALES
BYWARD ST
33C
City Hall
Number 7 view
32
Tower Pier
LOWER THAMES ST
GREAT TOWER ST
ABBOTS LANE
MORGAN'S LANE
HMS Belfast
MORE LONDON PLACE
TOOLEY STREET
Shard view
IDOL LN
ST MARY AT HILL
Hay's Galleria
HAY'S LANE
London Bridge City Pier
LOWER THAMES ST
MONUMENT ST
London Bridge
31
The Shard
33E
LONDON BRIDGE
TOOLEY ST
DUKE ST HILL
RAILWAY APPROACH
LONDON BRIDGE ST
ST THOMAS STREET
SWAN LANE
London Bridge
ANGEL LANE

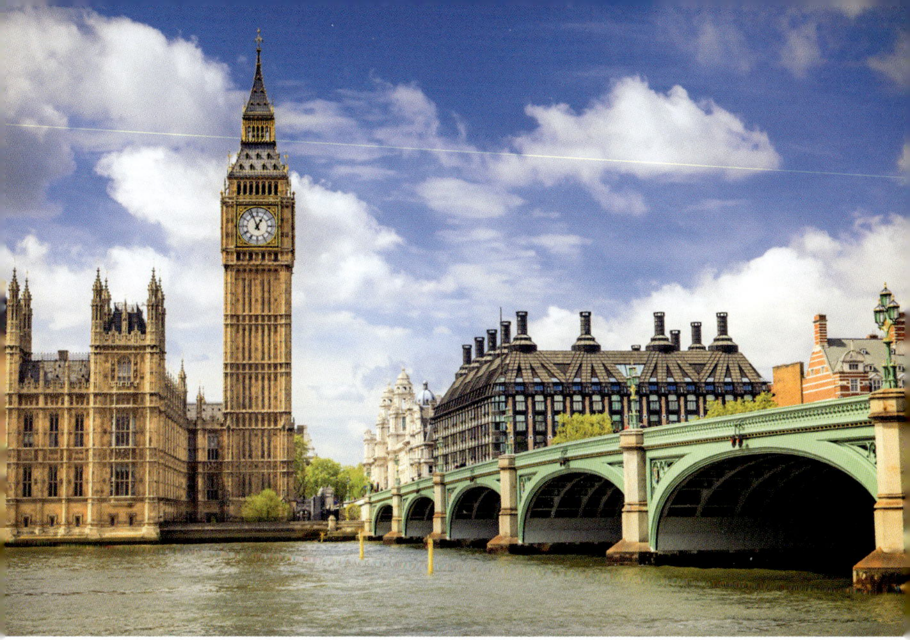

20 THE HOUSES OF PARLIAMENT & BIG BEN

There are plenty of great viewpoints from which to capture these iconic buildings. The first is from directly opposite on the Albert Embankment (point 20A on the map). From here you get a traditional composition looking straight across the river at the buildings, which is best when the Thames is still and they're reflected in perfect symmetry.

Next, try from beside Westminster Bridge on the southern side (point 20B on the map). From here you can include the bridge in your composition as well, which serves as a great leading line to Big Ben (pictured above). If you go into the tunnel that runs under the bridge there's an interesting shot looking out, using the archway to frame Big Ben. There's also an unusual composition from the gardens in front of St Thomas's Hospital, where there's a modern fountain you can use as foreground (point 20C on the map).

If you stand on the waterfront between Westminster Bridge and the London Eye (point 20D on the map) you get a classic shot of the buildings with the bridge running through the middle of the frame.

A final viewpoint I'd recommend is from Westminster Bridge itself (point 20E on the map). From the southern side of the bridge you can use the pavement and railings as leading lines to Big Ben. There are also some old–fashioned lampposts on the bridge, which add interest to any photo here. The northern side of the bridge is a perfect location for capturing light trails from passing traffic, with the buildings in the background (pictured below).

Good reflections really improve any photo taken looking across the Thames, so the best time to visit is when the wind is low and the water is still. As you're looking west from all of the viewpoints it's a particularly good location for sunset, although there's a great shot to be had here at any time of day. As you'd also expect it's a fantastic location at night.

During the day there are also plenty of opportunities to do close–up shots of the beautiful gothic facade of The Houses of Parliament, for example the western side is especially ornate and looks good photographed with the statue of Richard the 1st on his horse in front of it. (Don't forget a close–up of the top of Big Ben either. It's a bit cliche, but there's nothing wrong with that).

» Practical Information

Tube: Westminster, Waterloo

Pier: Westminster

Bus: 11, 12, 24, 148, 159, 453

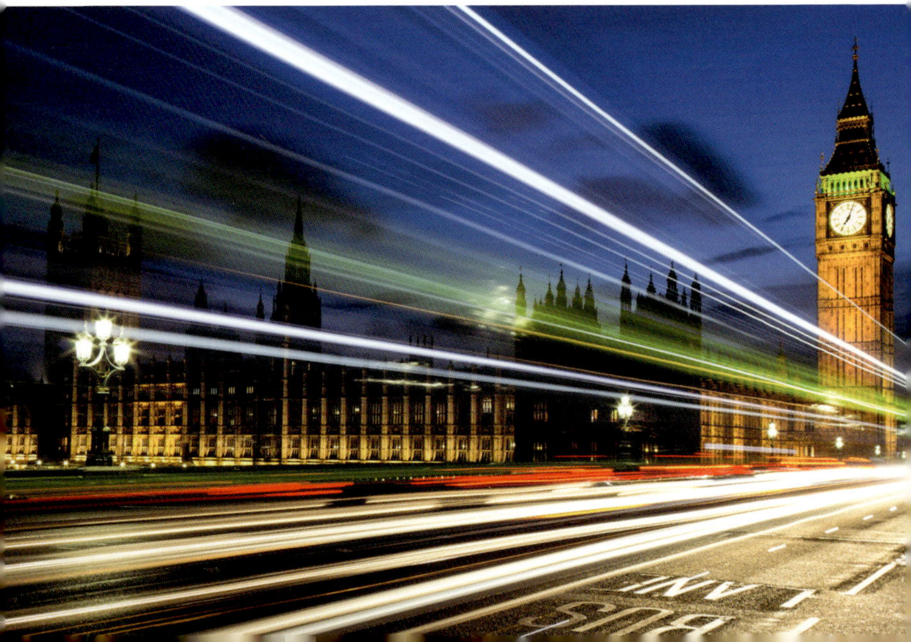

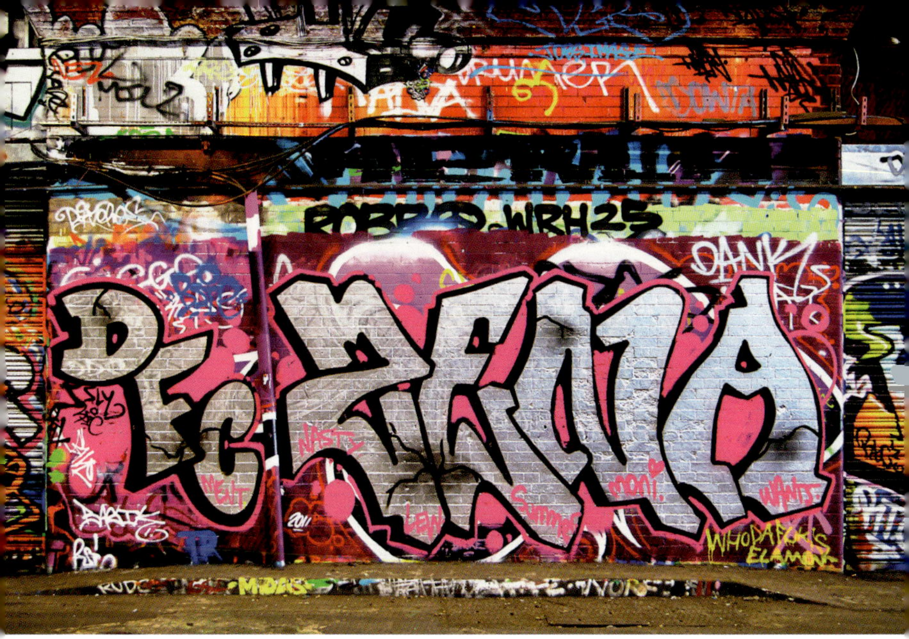

21 LEAKE STREET GRAFFITI TUNNEL

Leake Street graffiti tunnel is tucked away under the tracks of Waterloo Station, and as you've probably guessed from the name it's almost entirely covered with graffiti. It became an official area for graffiti during a street art festival in 2008, and remains a favourite haunt with many artists today. The artwork changes constantly so you never know what you might find, but close–up photos isolating attractive pieces or small sections of the tunnel wall work particularly well. The graffiti can be a bit chaotic, making it hard to get a clean composition, but there's plenty to choose from as it's around 200 metres long. Even on a bright day it can be pretty dark inside, which makes shooting hand–held quite tricky. If you have a tripod or anti–shake lens I'd recommend taking it. It does sometimes attract bored teenagers in the afternoon and can also be a bit eerie at night, so I'd advise visiting in the morning.

» Practical Information

Tube: Waterloo

Pier: London Eye

Bus: 76, 139, 188, 341, 381, RV1

22 THE LONDON EYE

The London Eye is one of the tallest Ferris wheels in the world and takes you up to a height of 135 metres, where you get a superb view over the rooftops in all directions. The view southwest over the Houses of Parliament is particularly good and photos that also include neighbouring capsules work especially well. Try to avoid going on just after it's rained though, as the water droplets on the outside of the capsules spoil most photos. Reflections on the glass can also be a problem, even on a dull day. Although the view is spectacular at night it's very difficult to photograph as the wheel constantly moves, so I wouldn't recommend this.

There are multiple viewpoints from which to capture the wheel itself. The first one I'd recommend is from Westminster Bridge (pictured on the right – point 22A on the map). From here you get a view of the wheel next to the beautiful Edwardian baroque County Hall building. The second viewpoint is from directly opposite the Eye on Victoria Embankment (pictured below – point 22B on the map), where you get a very

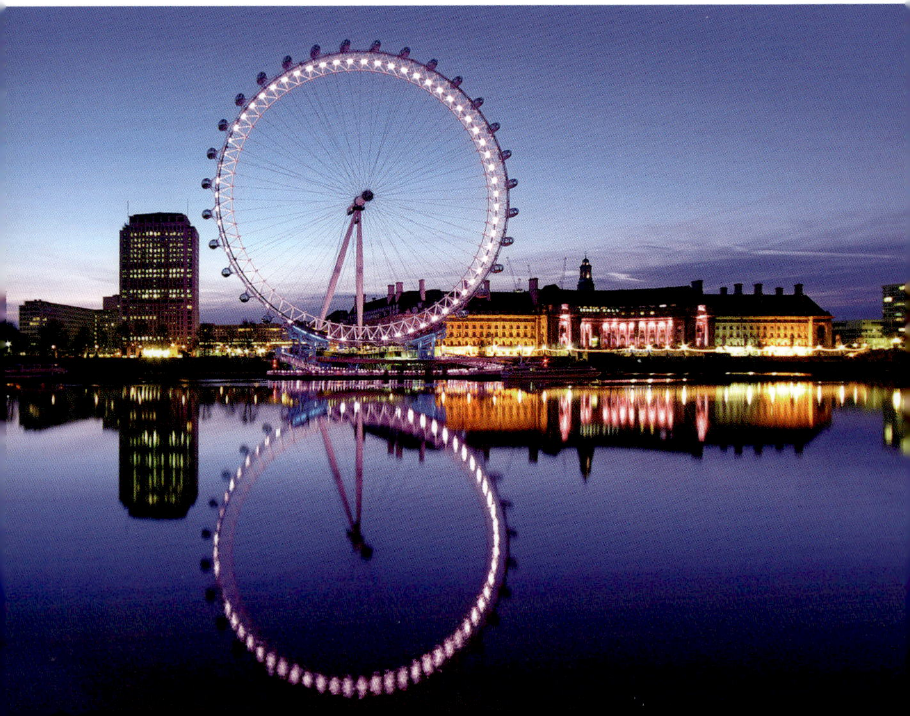

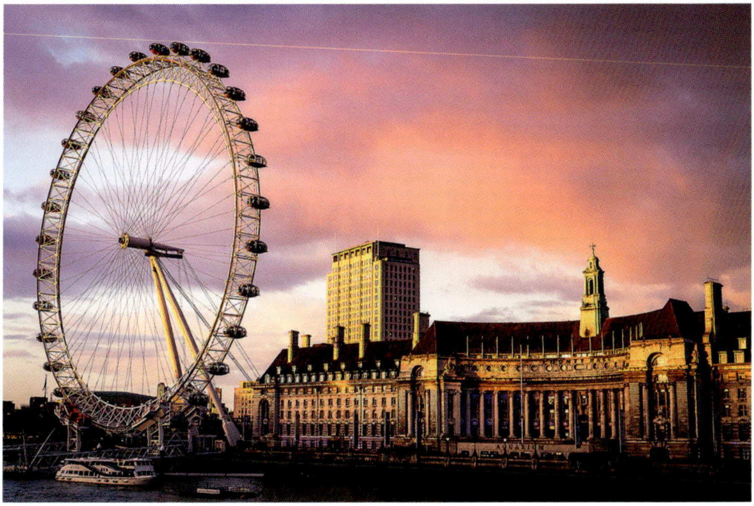

pleasing head–on perspective. Another good viewpoint is from Hungerford Bridge (point 22C on the map). From here there's a classic landscape shot with the Eye on the left and the Houses of Parliament on the right. Also, try from the tree lined avenue in Jubilee Gardens (point 22D on the map), looking along the avenue to the wheel behind. All these views are good during the day, but really come into their own at night, especially if the Thames is still. Finally, from the foot of the wheel there are lots of opportunities for abstract photos of the wheel set against the sky (pictured on the right).

» Practical Information

Tube: Waterloo, Westminster, Embankment

Pier: London Eye

Bus: 211, 77, 381, RV1

Web: www.londoneye.com

Tel: 0870 990 8883

Open: 10am – 8.30/9.30pm

Closed: 25th December and one week in January for annual maintenance

Admission: From £20 for adults, £15 for children

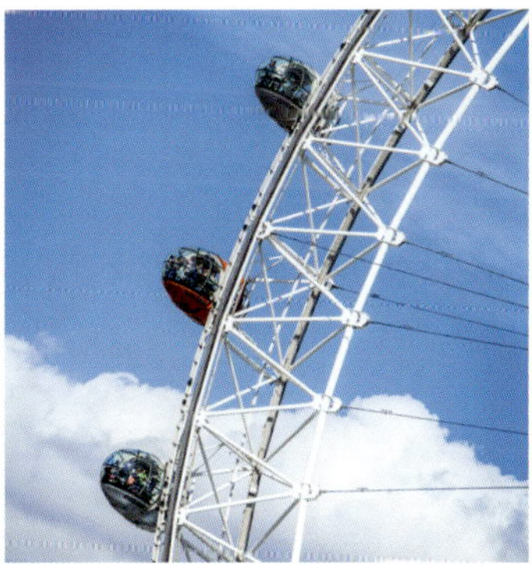

23 SOUTHBANK SKATE PARK

Nestled under the Southbank Centre, right on the Thames waterfront promenade, is the Southbank Skate Park. It's been an important venue in London's skateboarding scene for more than 40 years, although it's also popular with BMX riders and rollerbladers. It consists of a sunken area containing concrete ledges, bankings, stairs and pillars. Almost every surface in it is also adorned with graffiti. There are plenty of different compositions to explore here, such as close–up shots of the graffiti, wider shots taking in the atmosphere of the park (pictured below), or action shots if there are some skateboarders there when you visit. (If there are people skating then I'd recommend staying behind the railings for your own safety.) The best time to find it empty is on weekdays or early morning on the weekends. If you're after action shots then you'll find it busiest on weekend afternoons and anytime during the school holidays.

» Practical Information

Tube: Waterloo, Embankment

Pier: Festival

Bus: 1, 4, 26, 59, 68, 139, 168, 172, RV1

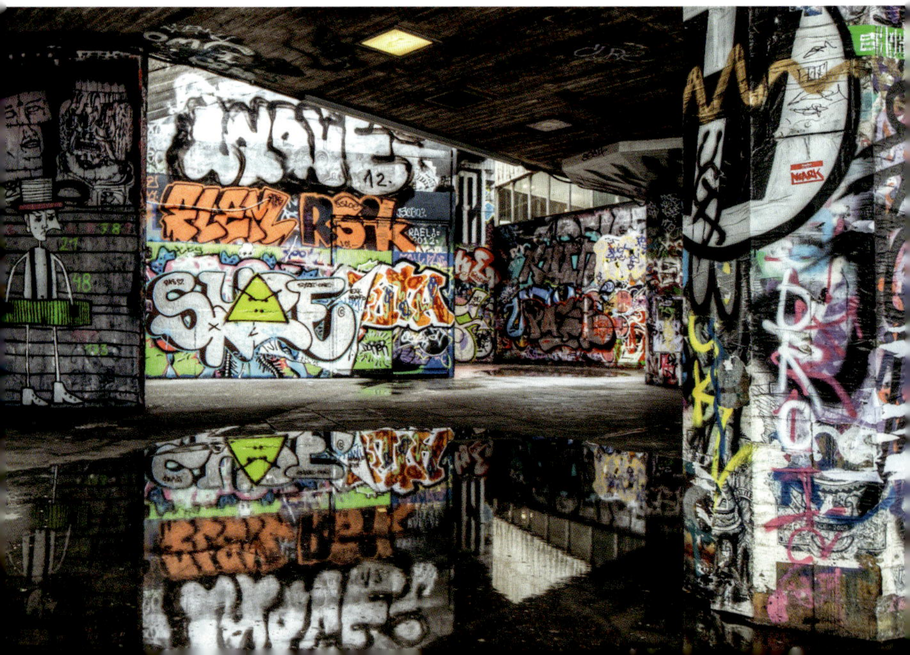

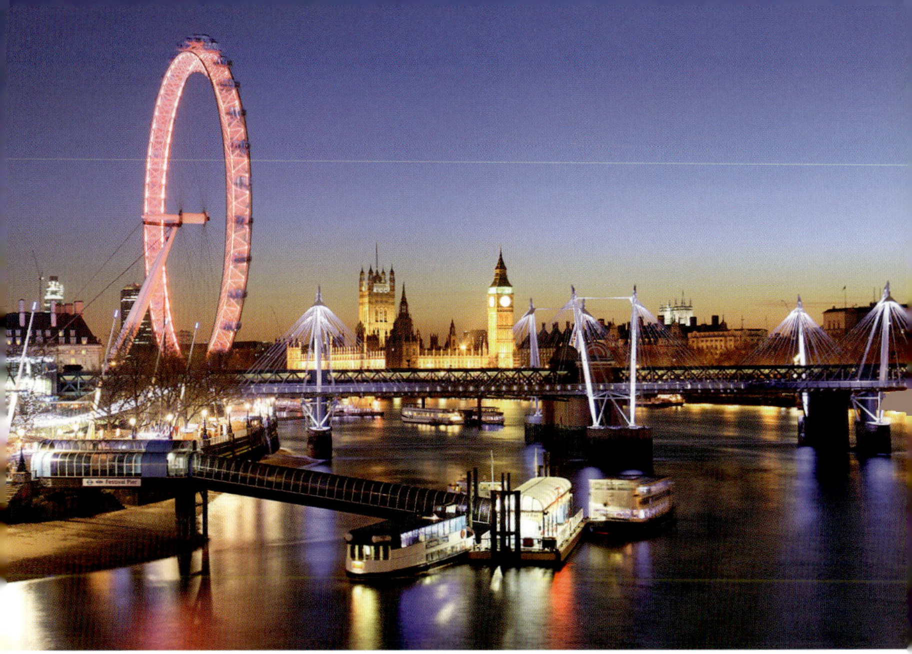

24 THE VIEW FROM WATERLOO BRIDGE

You get pretty good views from a lot of the bridges in central London, but Waterloo Bridge is a favourite location with many photographers. The classic view from here is looking southwest with the Houses of Parliament in the background, the London Eye and Hungerford Bridge in the midground, and Festival Pier in the foreground (pictured above). The view from the opposite side of the bridge looking east isn't quite as good as it lacks foreground, but is worth exploring while you're there. You get a clear view across the water to St Paul's and the skyscrapers of the City, as well as to Blackfriars Bridge and the Oxo Tower. This view works particularly well in panoramic format. The best time to visit is at night, but it's also a good location for sunrise (looking east) or sunset (looking west).

» Practical Information

Tube: Embankment, Waterloo, Temple

Pier: Festival, Embankment

Bus: 1, 4, 26, 59, 68, 138, 139, 168, 172, RV1

25 THE VIEW FROM THE OXO TOWER

The Oxo Tower was originally a power station, but was bought and rebuilt in the 1920s by the makers of Oxo stock cubes, who incorporated the recognisable "OXO" windows at the top of the tower. It's now a mixture of shops, galleries, flats and restaurants. It's also one of the few buildings in London with a viewing gallery open to the public. On the eighth floor there's a restaurant with a large balcony that overlooks the Thames – a small part of this balcony is open to the public. From here you get a great view looking northeast over Blackfriars Bridge towards St Paul's (pictured below). The view is best at night and tripods are allowed.

» Practical Information

Tube: Blackfriars, Southwark, Waterloo

Pier: Blackfriars

Bus: RV1, 381

Getting to the public gallery: From the waterfront, follow the signs for the lift and take it to the 8th floor. Ask at the restaurant reception where the public viewing gallery is and they will show you the way.

Open: It's only accessible when the lifts are running, which is around the restaurant opening hours (it doesn't open until noon, but the lifts usually run from about 9 am to midnight).

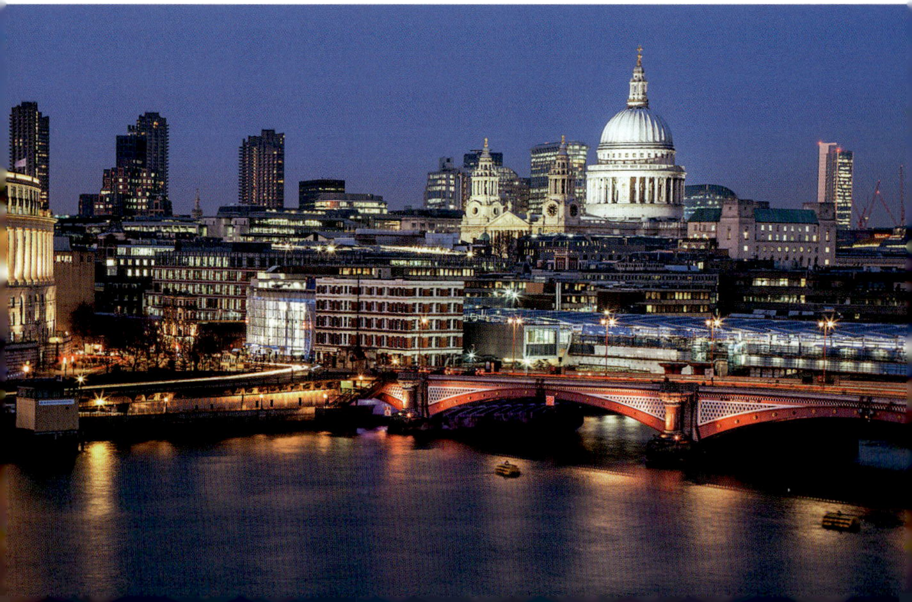

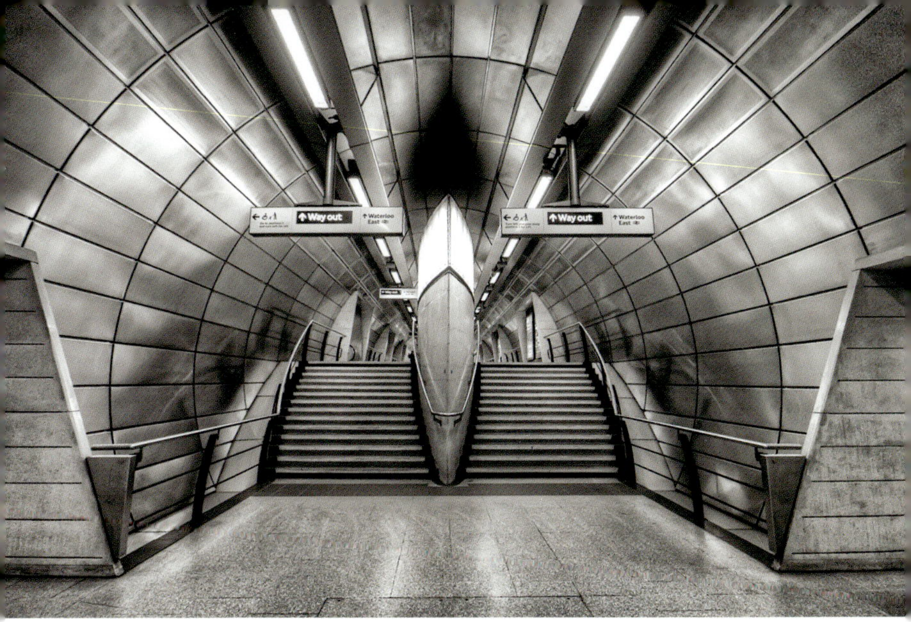

26 SOUTHWARK TUBE STATION

This modern tube station on the Jubilee line has a very futuristic feel to it, with clean lines and walls clad in stainless steel panels. Between the two platforms on the lower concourse you'll find a striking scene by the steps at either end (pictured above). Also, the escalators that link the upper and lower concourses are interesting to shoot – make sure you investigate the escalator entrances as well as the tunnels themselves, which look great photographed from the top as you're going down or from the bottom as you're going up. Another feature to explore is the huge blue glass panelled wall on the upper concourse. You can get some unusual shots here by capturing passing commuters reflected in the glass. You aren't allowed to use tripods or flash in tube stations, so you'll need steady hands to shoot on the escalators or the lower concourse, as they're both quite dark (the upper concourse has a glass roof to let light in so is less of a problem).

» Practical Information

Tube: Southwark

Bus: 45, 63, 100, N63, N89

See page 105 for important information about taking photos in tube stations.

27 THE MILLENNIUM BRIDGE

This beautiful steel suspension bridge was built to commemorate the millennium in 2000. The view from the southern bank of the Thames looking across it towards St Paul's is probably one of the most photographed in London (pictured below). It's best at night and there's plenty of room along the riverside promenade to get a composition you like (try from the left and the right side of the bridge, as both give an equally good view). The second location to explore is the very southern end of the bridge, where the railings of the bridge can be used as leading lines towards St Paul's (pictured bottom right). This works best if you can get the dome exactly in the centre of the frame and include some of the ramp leading up onto the bridge. There's a similar but equally good composition from the middle of the bridge (pictured top right). Again, more symmetrical shots tend to work better so aim to get St Paul's in the centre of the railings. Also, if you look southeast from this point you'll get a great view of the Shard. Lastly, make sure you check out the view from the northern side of the bridge, looking south towards the Tate Modern. The bridge is busy during

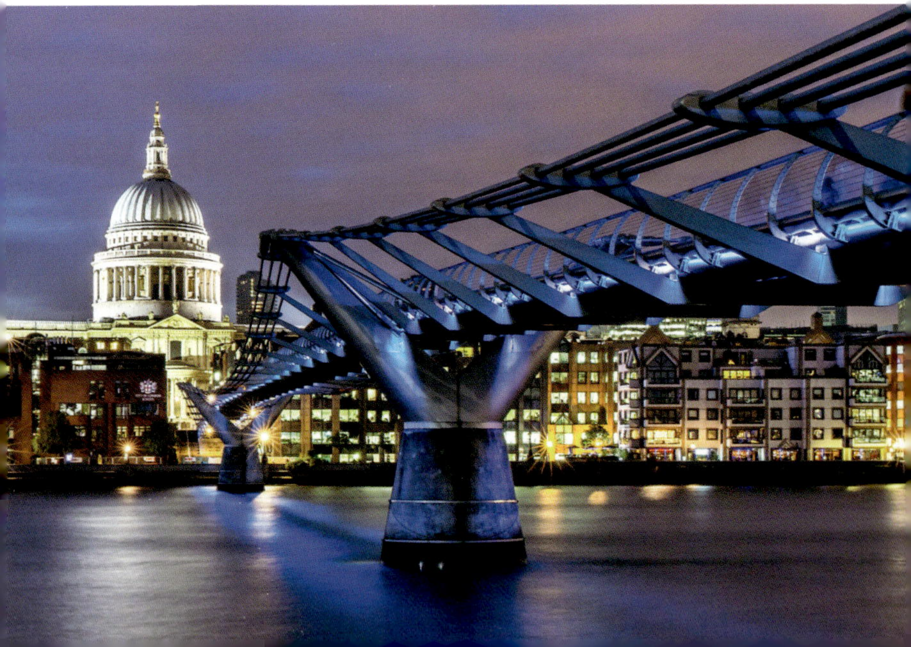

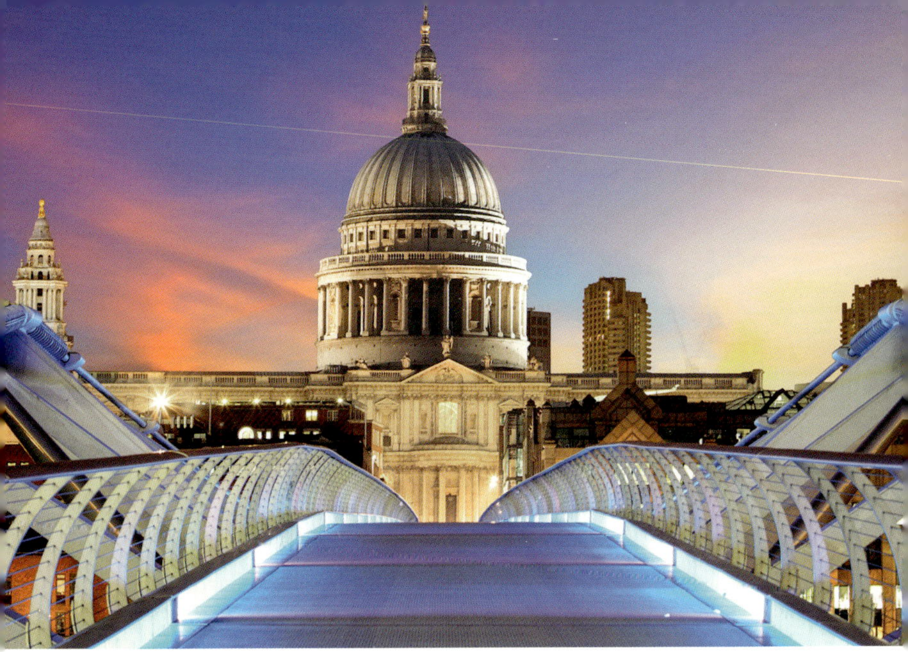

the day, so if you want to shoot it without people on it's best to visit early or late. Also, if you're using a tripod beware of vibrations from people walking past.

» Practical Information

Tube: Southwark, Blackfriars

Pier: Bankside

Bus: 45, 63, 100, RV1, 381, 344

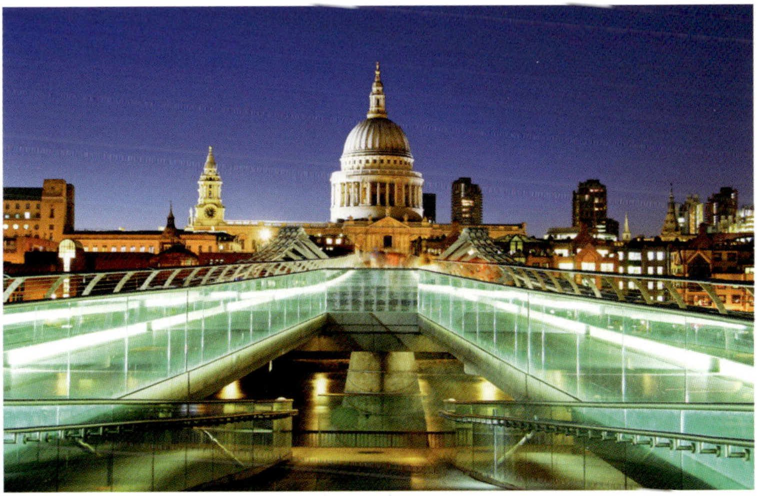

28 TATE MODERN

This popular modern art gallery is housed in an old power station right beside the Thames. It's a great place for street photography as you can get some really interesting shots of people studying the art on display in the stark interior. A particularly good spot for this is the vast Turbine Hall, which often houses giant art installations. Even when the hall is empty it's still interesting to shoot people walking through it (pictured on the right). It's best in strong afternoon light and there's a great vantage point to shoot from on level 1.

Also, on level 3 there's an outside balcony with an excellent view over the Thames and the Millennium Bridge towards St Paul's (head for the small cafe and you'll find it). If you venture up to the restaurant on level 6 you get a similar view, but from higher up and behind glass. Another interesting composition on this level is to shoot the people sat at the windows silhouetted against the view.

» Practical Information

Tube: Southwark, Blackfriars,
Pier: Bankside

Bus: 45, 63, 100, RV1, 381, 344

Web: www.tate.org.uk

Tel: 020 7887 8888

Open: 10am – 6pm Sunday to Thursday, 10am – 10pm Friday and Saturday

Closed: 24th–26th December

Admission: Free

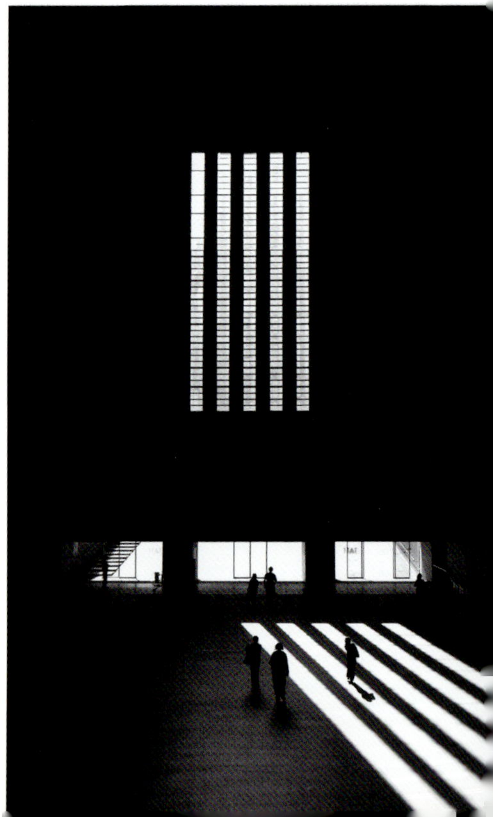

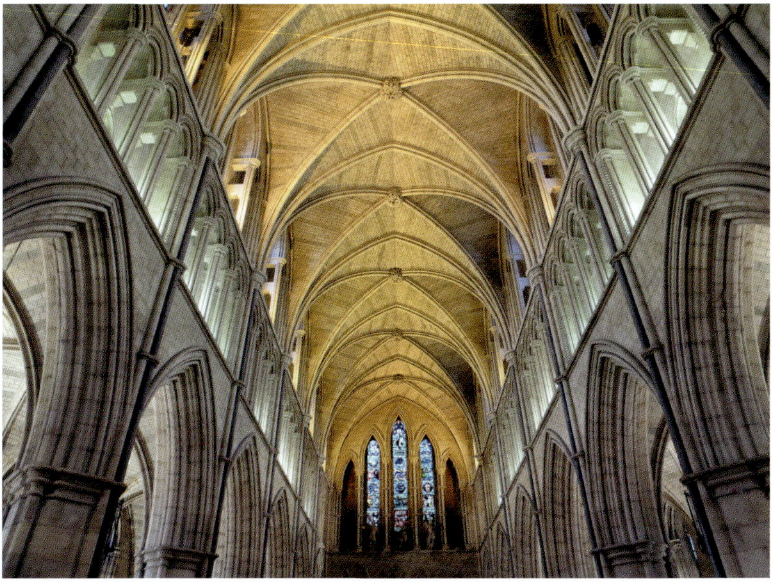

29 SOUTHWARK CATHEDRAL

This small cathedral near London Bridge has been a place of worship for over 1000 years. From the outside it's rather unremarkable, but inside it's an architectural delight. The most interesting feature is the fantastic rib-vaulted ceiling of the nave (pictured above). Along with this there are plenty of other subjects to do detail shots of, such as the stained-glass windows and the wrought iron chandeliers. It can be quite dark inside, so if you have a tripod you might want to take it with you (tripods are allowed as long as they're used considerately).

» Practical Information

Tube: London Bridge

Pier: London Bridge City

Bus: 17, 21, 35, 40, 43, 45, 47, 48, 133, 141, 149, 381, 521, RV1

Web: cathedral.southwark.anglican.org

Tel: 020 7367 6700

Open: 10am – 5pm

Closed: 25th December

Admission: Free, but you'll need to purchase a photography permit from the shop to shoot inside (£2.50 at the time of writing).

30 BOROUGH MARKET

Hidden away under the railway arches near London Bridge Station is Borough Market – one of London's largest and oldest food markets. It offers fine British produce as well as speciality foods from all over the world. Along with fresh fruit and veg you'll find stalls selling cheese, fish, bread, cakes, meat, game and delicious lunchtime snacks.

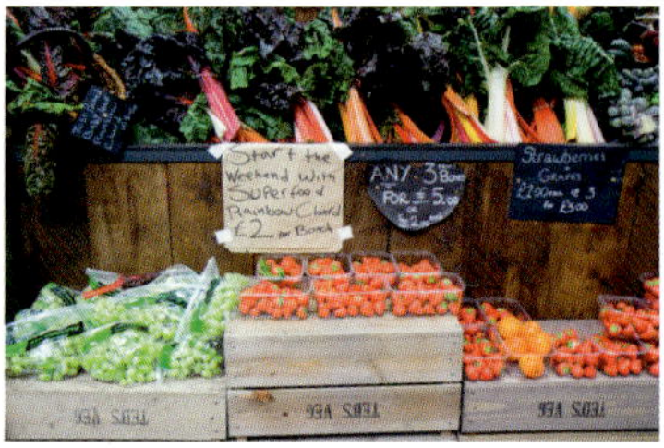

All the produce is beautifully displayed, so there's always plenty to photograph – filling the frame with particularly colourful arrangements or isolating interesting produce usually works well. Alternatively, it's a great place for street photography as locals and tourists alike wander around browsing the delicacies on offer. Some stalls are open on Mondays and Tuesdays, but the best time to visit is on a full market day (Wednesday to Saturday) when all the stalls are open and the market is a hive of activity.

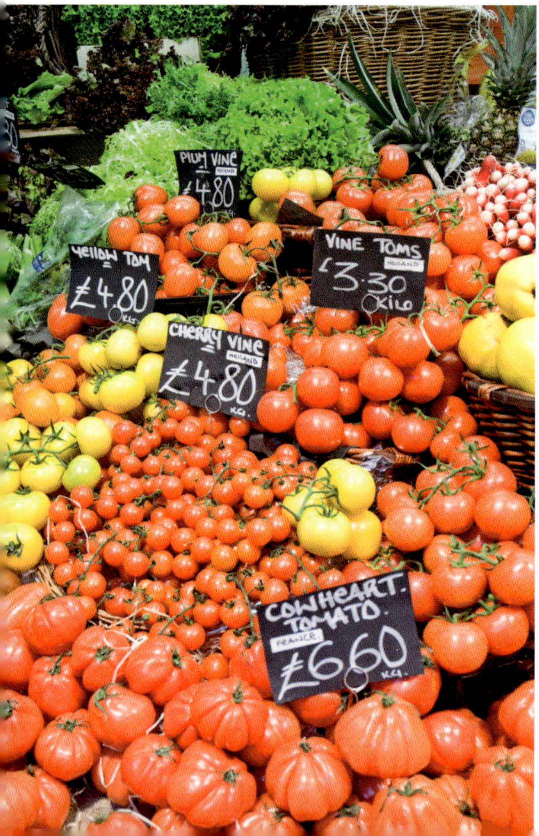

» Practical Information

Tube: London Bridge

Pier: London Bridge City

Bus: 21, 35, 40, 43, 133, 141, 149, 343, 381, 521, RV1

Web: www.boroughmarket.org.uk

Open: Monday to Thursday 10am – 5pm, Friday 10am – 6pm, Saturday 8am – 5pm.

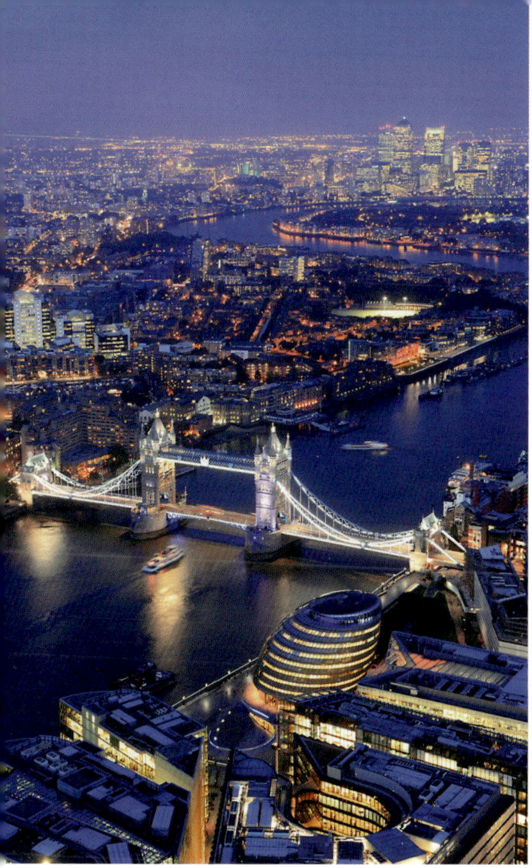

31 THE VIEW FROM THE SHARD

The Shard is a striking building that can be seen on the skyline from many places in London, but it also houses a viewing gallery on the 69th and 72nd floors – a whopping 240 metres up. Despite being quite expensive to visit it is one of the best places to get a higher view of the city, and one of the few places you can do so at night. The 360° views are spectacular, particularly the view east over Tower Bridge towards Canary Wharf (pictured on the left). Your ticket allows you entry during a 30 minute time slot, but there's no restriction on how long you can stay, so the best tactic to get your money's worth is to go up just before sunset and then stay until it gets dark and the city lights up. Unfortunately tripods aren't allowed, making night photography quite tricky (if you have one with you you'll be asked to leave it at security). The only way to get around this is to take a bag, put it on the floor and balance your camera on top. The gallery is indoors, so glass reflections can also be a problem, especially on a bright day but also at night from the interior lights. Wearing dark clothing and shielding the glass with your body helps avoid them. It is very high up, so if you want to do close-up shots of particular buildings below you'll need a decent zoom on your camera or a mid-length lens.

» Practical Information

Tube: London Bridge

Pier: London Bridge City

Bus: 43, 48, 141, 149, 521

Web: theviewfromtheshard.com

Tel: 0844 499 7111

Open: April to October 10am – 10pm, November to March 10am – 7pm (10pm on Thursday, Friday and Saturday).

Closed: 25th December

Admission: £30 for adults, £24 for children

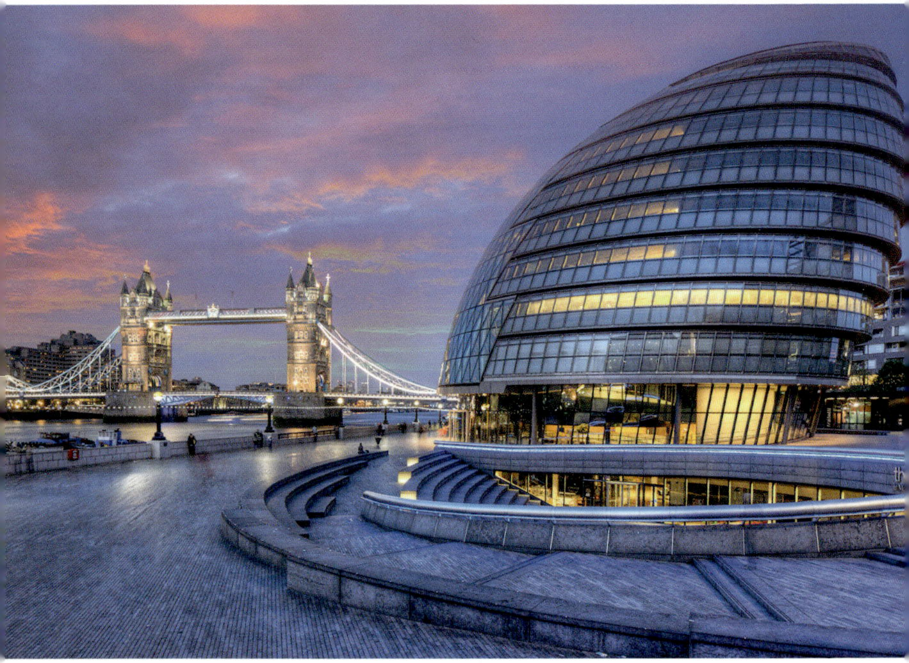

32 CITY HALL & MORE LONDON

City Hall is a very striking modern building right on the Thames waterfront. It's part of the "More London" development, which also includes offices, restaurants, shops and an outdoor amphitheatre called The Scoop.

One of the best views of City Hall is from the western side of the building, looking east with Tower Bridge in the background (pictured above). The stone steps and metal railings of the Scoop provide ample foreground and

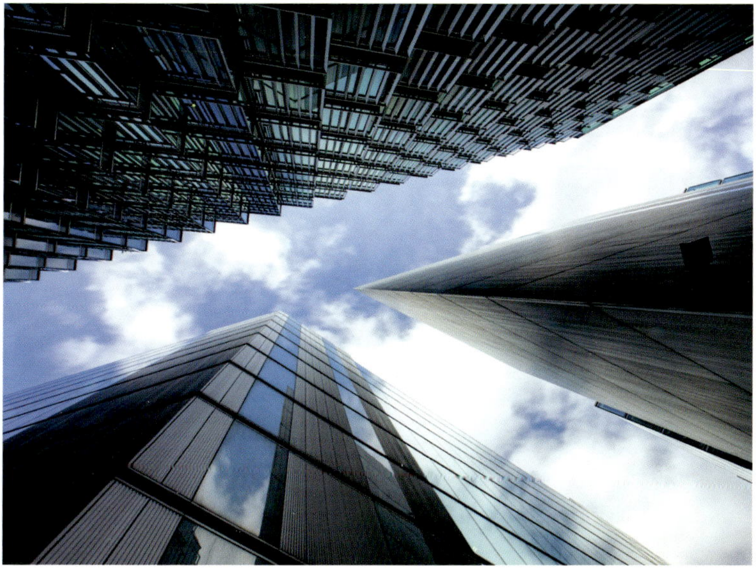

there are lots of different variations of the composition to explore. The Scoop is also a useful foreground element for compositions looking west towards the office blocks and the Shard.

As well as City Hall there are plenty of other subjects to photograph at More London. If you walk along the pedestrianised street that runs between the office blocks you get a great view of the Shard framed by the buildings either side. The striped paving also runs parallel to the buildings, creating useful leading lines. Midway along this street you'll find another interesting composition. If you look straight up you'll get an unusual view where three buildings converge to form a pleasing Y shape (pictured above). Finally, it's well worth investigating the "7 More London Riverside" building, which has an interesting curved glass front with bridges linking the two wings. The shape creates lots of unusual reflections and looks great captured from right in front of the entrance looking up.

The area is just as good to photograph during the day as it is at night and the City Hall view is also suitable for sunrise.

» Practical Information

Tube: London Bridge, Tower Hill

Pier: London Bridge City, Tower, St Katharine's

Bus: 42, 47, 78, 381, RV1

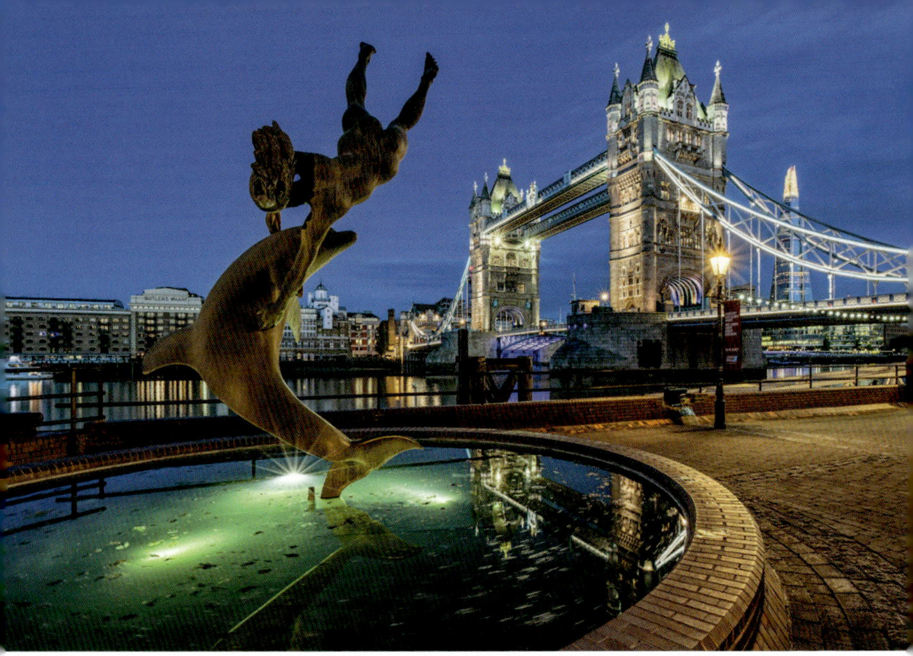

33 TOWER BRIDGE

There are plenty of different viewpoints from which to capture this iconic bridge. The first is from the northern bank of the Thames, on the waterfront next to the Tower of London (point 33A on the map). There's a clear view of the bridge from here however it lacks any kind of foreground. It's worth investigating if the water is still though and there's also a good view from here across the river to City Hall and the Shard.

The second viewpoint is also from the northern bank, but to the east of the bridge near St Katharine's Pier (point 33B on the map). Here you'll find the Girl with a Dolphin Fountain, which makes great foreground for the bridge behind (pictured above). If you walk a little further past this point you'll also find a huge sundial that can be used in the same way, and last but not least the pier can be used as foreground interest too.

The third location is from the bridge itself, where you can use the suspension cables and bridge railings to lead the eye to one of the towers. This looks particularly good at night with light trails from passing traffic (pictured on the right). If you look west from the bridge you also get a superb view of the Shard nestled behind City Hall and More London.

The next two locations are on the southern bank of the Thames. The first is from next to City Hall – point 33C on the map. Again there's little foreground here, but a wider shot including the waterfront railings and lampposts works well. The other viewpoint is from Butler's Wharf (point 33D on the map). If you walk down Shad Thames street you'll find a passageway on the left after about 100 metres that takes you to the waterfront. There's also a passageway just before that where you can actually get down onto the shore of the Thames (be aware of the tide if you do this though as it can come in quite quickly).

Finally, from London Bridge (point 33E on the map) you get a head–on view of Tower Bridge and you can also include HMS Belfast in the scene.

Since you can shoot from either the east or west of the bridge it's suitable for both sunrise and sunset. If you want to capture sunrise go to the western side and if you want to capture sunset go to the eastern side (although you can also get great shots the other way around by capturing the warm light as it hits the bridge instead of the sunrise or sunset behind it).

» Practical Information

Tube: Tower Hill, London Bridge

Pier: Tower, St Katharine's, London Bridge City

Bus: 42, 78, RV1

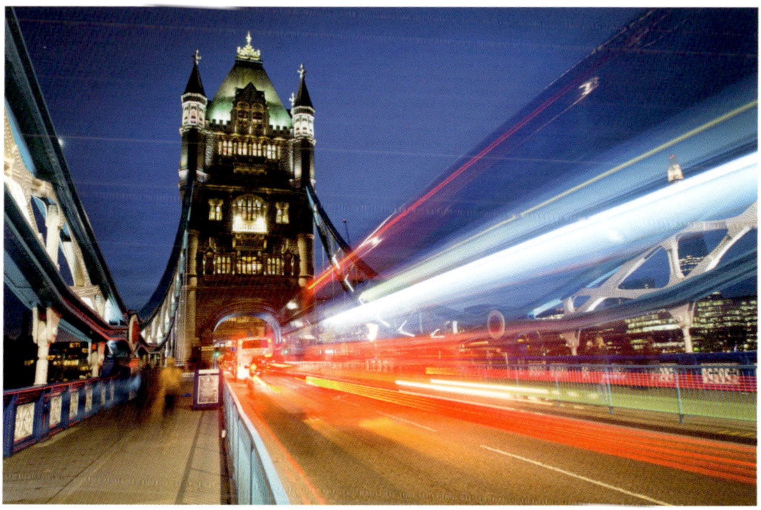

5 SECTION The City

The City is the oldest part of London and is also known locally as "the square mile". It's an important business and finance centre and has a fantastic mix of old and new architecture, with modern skyscrapers squeezed in among Georgian, Victorian and Gothic buildings. A few of the skyscrapers are notably photogenic, such as the Gherkin and the Lloyd's Building. Some of the taller buildings are also open to the public and have some great views. These include The Monument to The Great Fire of London and the Sky Garden at the top of 20 Fenchurch Street. (See page 100 for a couple more high views in the City.)

The City is also home to one of London's most iconic landmarks – St Paul's Cathedral. This is a must–visit location for any photographer as there are so many great viewpoints to shoot it from. If you're feeling energetic the view from the top is also quite spectacular. Nearby is Paternoster Square, which is well worth a look if you're in the area.

The area has over 50 old churches, such as Temple Church and the now ruined St Dunstan in the East. If you're interested in photographing church interiors there are many others in the City, see pages 101–102 for some suggestions.

At the end of this section I've included three locations just to the east of the City – the famous Tower of London, Brick Lane (which is a great place to photograph street art and also has a market) and Columbia Road Flower Market. If you're in the area for the day and fancy checking out some more markets there's also Petticoat Lane Market and Old Spitalfields Market (see pages 100–101 for more).

The City is a lot quieter at the weekends than it is during the week, so it's usually a better time to visit. The exceptions to this are the Tower of London, which is one of London's most popular tourist attractions so busy most of the time, and the markets in the East End, which fill the streets on a Sunday. Many of the locations are just as good to photograph during the day as they are at night. If you're visiting at night, the Bank area is also worth exploring, especially the Royal Exchange building. Please note that locations 36 and 37 are unfortunately not accessible by wheelchair.

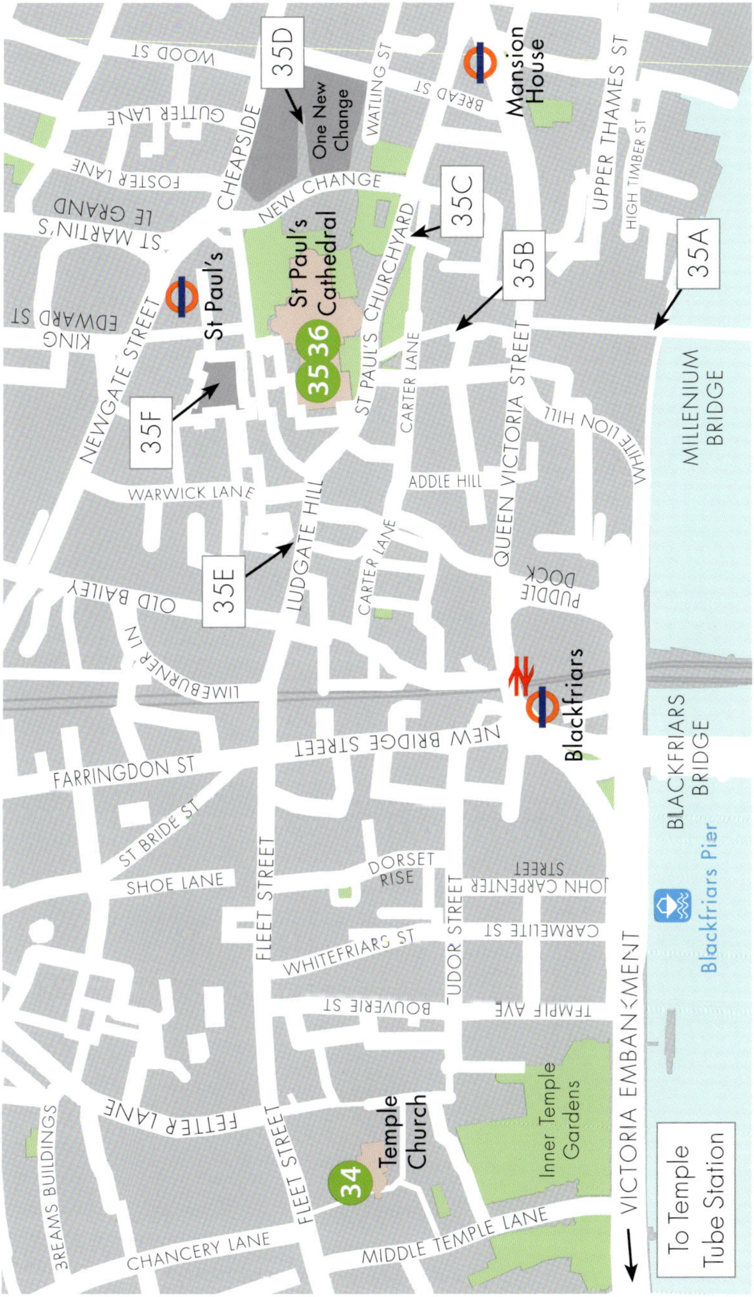
WOOD ST
GUTTER LANE
FOSTER LANE
ST MARTIN'S LE GRAND
CHEAPSIDE
35D
One New Change
WATLING ST
BREAD ST
Mansion House
NEW CHANGE
St Paul's Cathedral
ST PAUL'S CHURCHYARD
35C
UPPER THAMES ST
HIGH TIMBER ST
35B
35A
KING EDWARD ST
NEWGATE STREET
St Paul's
35
36
35F
CARTER LANE
QUEEN VICTORIA STREET
WHITE LION HILL
MILLENIUM BRIDGE
WARWICK LANE
ADDLE HILL
LUDGATE HILL
35E
OLD BAILEY
CARTER LANE
PUDDLE DOCK
LIMEBURNER LN
Blackfriars
NEW BRIDGE STREET
FARRINGDON ST
BLACKFRIARS BRIDGE
ST BRIDE ST
SHOE LANE
FLEET STREET
DORSET RISE
JOHN CARPENTER STREET
Blackfriars Pier
WHITEFRIARS ST
TUDOR STREET
CARMELITE ST
BOUVERIE ST
TEMPLE AVE
VICTORIA EMBANKMENT
FETTER LANE
Inner Temple Gardens
Temple Church
34
FLEET STREET
3REAMS BUILDINGS
CHANCERY LANE
MIDDLE TEMPLE LANE
To Temple Tube Station

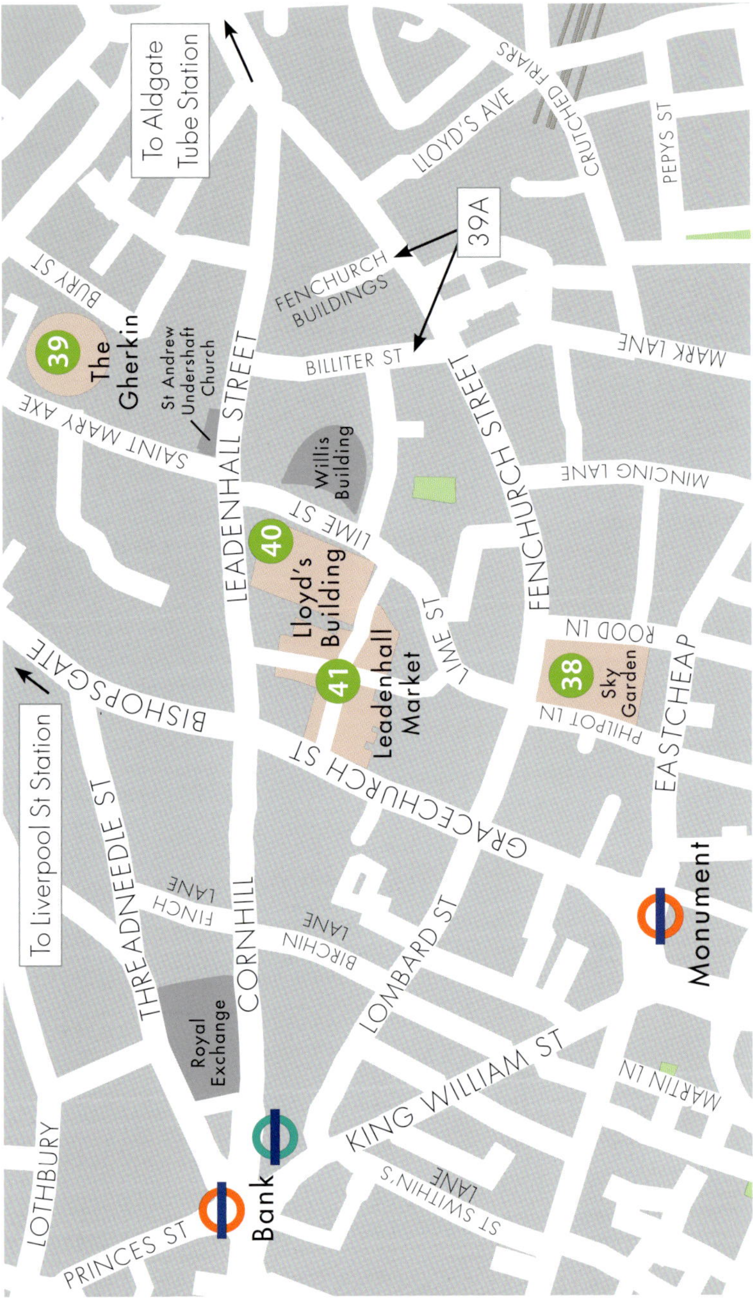
To Aldgate Tube Station
To Liverpool St Station
39 The Gherkin
St Andrew Undershaft Church
40 Lloyd's Building
41 Leadenhall Market
38 Sky Garden
Willis Building
Royal Exchange
39A
Bank
Monument
BURY ST
SAINT MARY AXE
LEADENHALL STREET
FENCHURCH BUILDINGS
BILLITER ST
LLOYD'S AVE
CRUTCHED FRIARS
PEPYS ST
MARK LANE
MINCING LANE
FENCHURCH STREET
LIME ST
ROOD LN
PHILPOT LN
EASTCHEAP
BISHOPSGATE
GRACECHURCH ST
THREADNEEDLE ST
FINCH LANE
CORNHILL
BIRCHIN LANE
LOMBARD ST
KING WILLIAM ST
MARTIN LN
ST SWITHIN'S LANE
LOTHBURY
PRINCES ST

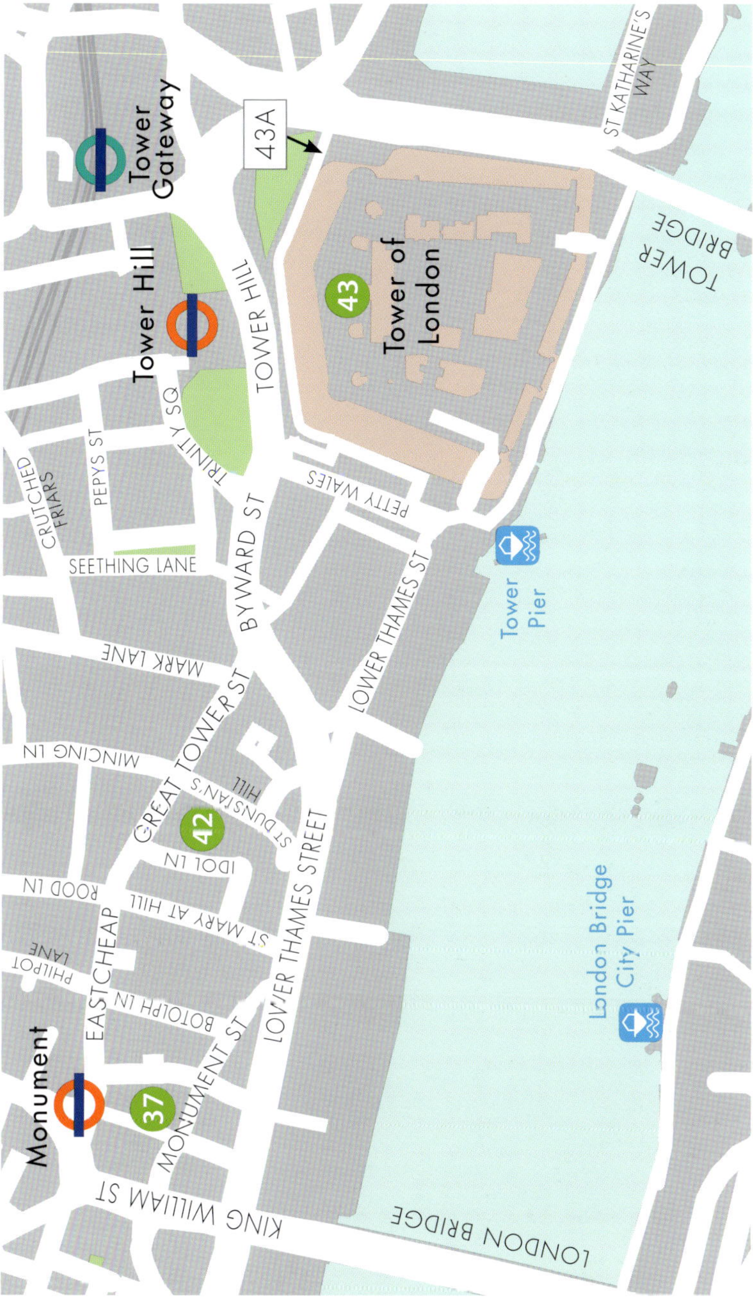
Tower Gateway
Tower Hill
TOWER HILL
43A
43
Tower of London
TOWER BRIDGE
ST KATHARINE'S WAY
TRINITY SQ
CRUTCHED FRIARS
PEPYS ST
PETTY WALES
SEETHING LANE
BYWARD ST
LOWER THAMES ST
Tower Pier
MARK LANE
GREAT TOWER ST
MINCING LN
ST DUNSTAN'S HILL
42
IDOL LN
ROOD LN
ST MARY AT HILL
EASTCHEAP
PHILPOT LANE
BOTOLPH LN
LOWER THAMES STREET
London Bridge City Pier
Monument
37
MONUMENT ST
KING WILLIAM ST
LONDON BRIDGE

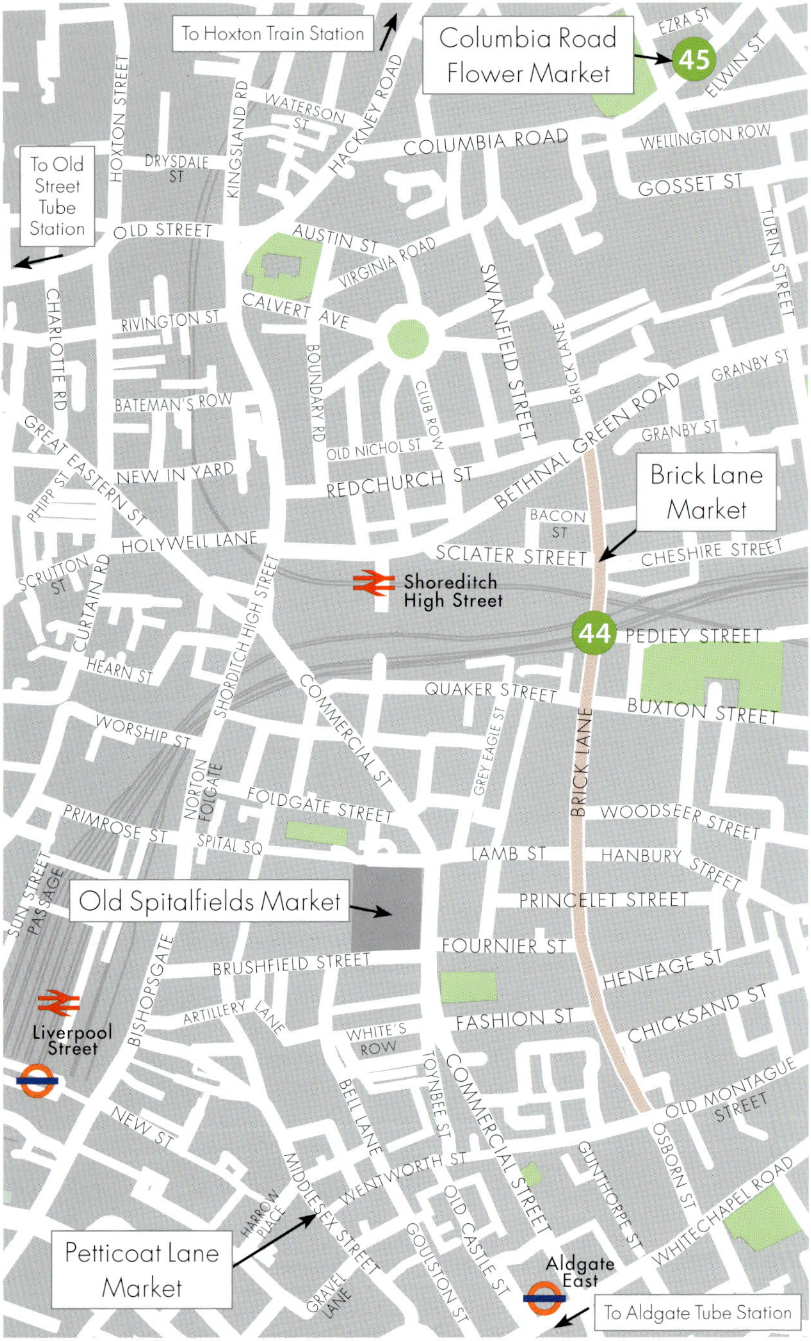
To Hoxton Train Station
Columbia Road Flower Market
45
EZRA ST
ELWIN ST
WATERSON ST
HACKNEY ROAD
KINGSLAND RD
HOXTON STREET
DRYSDALE ST
COLUMBIA ROAD
WELLINGTON ROW
GOSSET ST
To Old Street Tube Station
OLD STREET
AUSTIN ST
VIRGINIA ROAD
TURIN STREET
CALVERT AVE
CHARLOTTE RD
RIVINGTON ST
SWANFIELD STREET
BRICK LANE
BOUNDARY RD
CLUB ROW
GRANBY ST
BATEMAN'S ROW
BETHNAL GREEN ROAD
OLD NICHOL ST
GREAT EASTERN ST
NEW IN YARD
REDCHURCH ST
Brick Lane Market
PHIPP ST
BACON ST
HOLYWELL LANE
SCLATER STREET
CHESHIRE STREET
SCRUTTON ST
CURTAIN RD
Shoreditch High Street
SHOREDITCH HIGH STREET
44
PEDLEY STREET
HEARN ST
COMMERCIAL ST
QUAKER STREET
BUXTON STREET
WORSHIP ST
GREY EAGLE ST
NORTON FOLGATE
FOLGATE STREET
WOODSEER STREET
PRIMROSE ST
SPITAL SQ
LAMB ST
HANBURY STREET
SUN STREET PASSAGE
Old Spitalfields Market
PRINCELET STREET
FOURNIER ST
BISHOPSGATE
BRUSHFIELD STREET
HENEAGE ST
ARTILLERY LANE
FASHION ST
CHICKSAND ST
Liverpool Street
WHITE'S ROW
TOYNBEE ST
COMMERCIAL STREET
OLD MONTAGUE STREET
BELL LANE
NEW ST
OSBORN ST
GUNTHORPE ST
WENTWORTH ST
MIDDLESEX STREET
HARROW PLACE
OLD CASTLE ST
WHITECHAPEL ROAD
Petticoat Lane Market
GOULSTON ST
GRAVEL LANE
Aldgate East
To Aldgate Tube Station

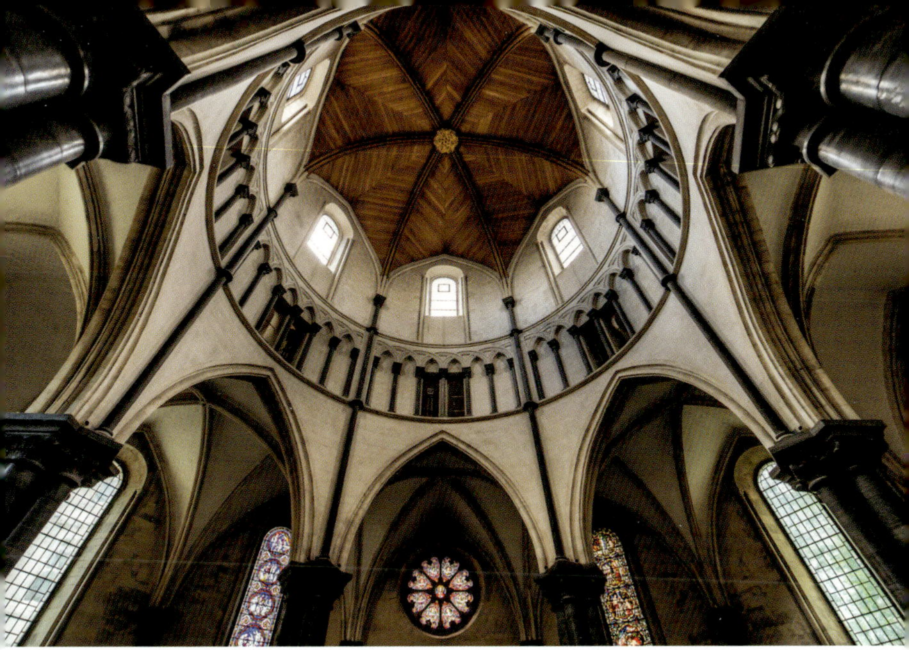

34 TEMPLE CHURCH

Tucked away behind Fleet Street is this 12th Century church, which was built by the Nights Templar as their headquarters. The decoration inside is less ornate than in many other London churches, but the stunning architecture more than makes up for this. It has an unusual circular nave and the chancel is filled with dark marble columns that lead upwards to gothic arches and a beautiful rib-vaulted ceiling. The ceiling of the nave is also particularly photogenic (pictured above) – a popular abstract composition of it is from right in the middle, looking straight up. There are also some elaborate stained–glass windows to do detail shots of. If you want to use a tripod inside you can but there's an extra cost (£25, payable at the welcome desk).

» Practical Information

Tube: Temple, Blackfriars

Bus: 4, 11, 15, 23, 26, 76, 341

Web: www.templechurch.com

Tel: 020 7353 3470

Open: 10am – 4pm Monday, Tuesday, Thursday, Friday, 2pm – 4pm Wednesday. (Times often change due to events, so check the website before visiting.)

Closed: Saturday and Sunday

Admission: £5 for adults, free for children

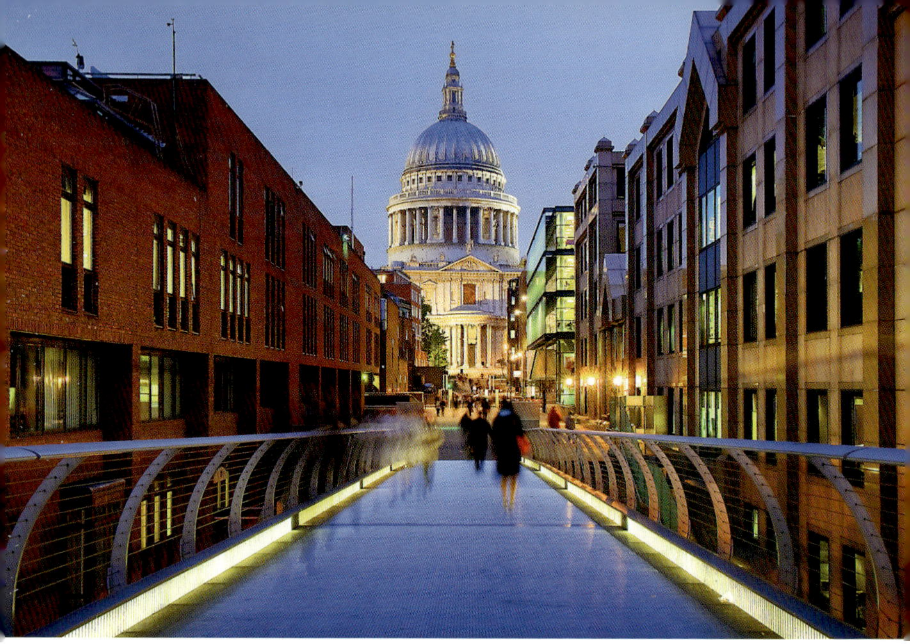

35 ST PAUL'S CATHEDRAL

This is one of the most impressive buildings in London and has dominated the skyline for over 300 years. Photography isn't allowed inside, but as well as views of it from the Millennium Bridge (see p53) there are plenty of other viewpoints to shoot the exterior from.

The first viewpoint is from the northern end of the Millennium Bridge, where the railings lead your eye towards the dome and the buildings on either side frame the scene perfectly (pictured above – point 35A on the map). The second viewpoint is from a little further north on the same street where a series of steps create wonderful leading lines to the cathedral (pictured below – point 35B on the map). If you

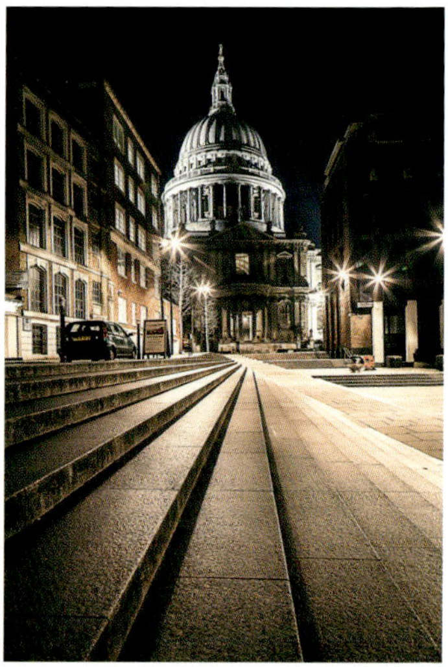

want to photograph the cathedral with light trails from passing traffic in front the best spot is on St Paul's Churchyard Street to the southeast (point 35C on the map).

To the east of the building are two further viewpoints, both at the One New Change shopping centre (point 35D on the map). The first of these is from the entrance to the shopping centre on New Change Street. If you look out from here you get an interesting composition of St Paul's reflected in the glass of the shopping centre windows (pictured below). This view is best during daylight as the reflections generally aren't as good when it gets dark. The shopping centre also has a public roof terrace where you get a fantastic view of the dome. It's a great spot for sunset and has a good view towards the Shard as well.

If you want to take in the grand front entrance to St Paul's (on the western side) a good place to try is from near the top of Ludgate Hill – point 35E on the map. Finally, there's also an interesting view of the dome from Paternoster Square, which lies to the north – point 35F on the map. The square is also interesting to photograph as a subject in itself.

» Practical Information

Tube: St Paul's, Mansion House, Blackfriars

Bus: 4, 11, 15, 23, 25, 26, 100, 242

One New Change roof terrace: Open 10am til late

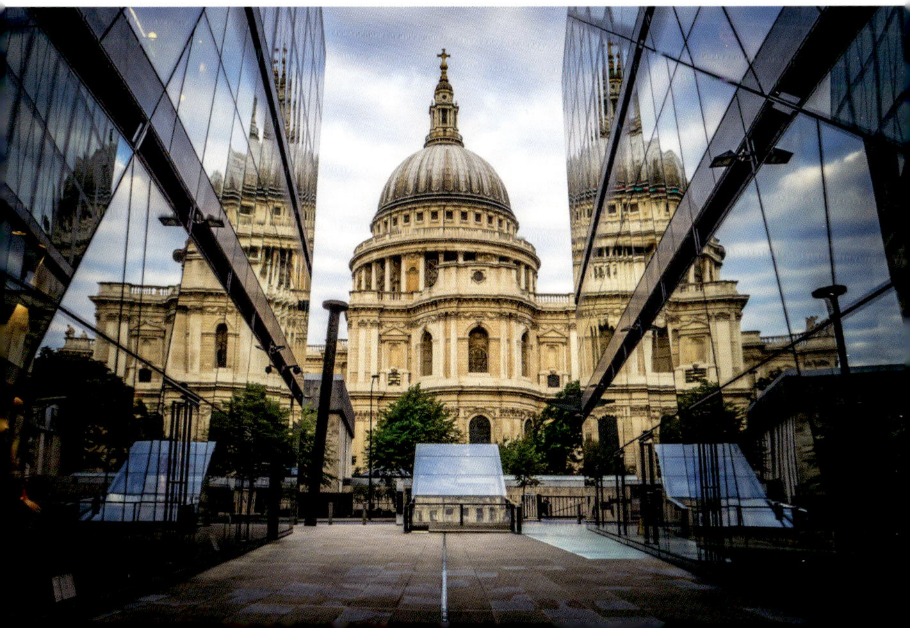

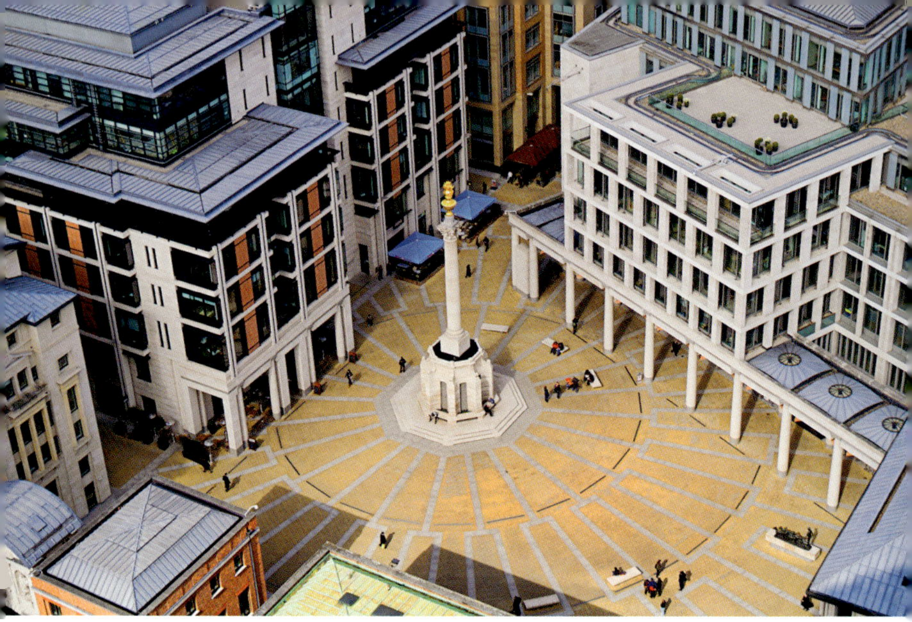

36 THE VIEW FROM ST PAUL'S

There are two balconies on the dome of St Paul's that both have 360° views of the city. From the lower balcony (called the Stone Gallery) there's a particularly good view west over the towers at the front of the cathedral, which is best at sunset. Looking east to the City skyscrapers is equally good and there's also an interesting perspective of Paternoster Square (pictured above). If you're happy to climb another 150 steps then continue up to the Golden Gallery at the very top. The view from here takes in all the same sights just from another 30 metres up. The spiral stairs up to both balconies are steep and narrow, so not recommended if you have heart problems, breathing problems or a fear of confined spaces. Also, tripods aren't allowed on the balconies.

» Practical Information

Tube: St Paul's, Mansion House, Blackfriars

Bus: 4, 11, 15, 23, 25, 26, 100, 242

Web: www.stpauls.co.uk

Tel: 020 7246 8350

Open: 8.30am – 4.30pm Monday to Saturday

Closed: Sundays

Admission: £17 for adults, £7.50 for children

37 THE VIEW FROM THE MONUMENT

The Monument to the Great Fire of London (commonly known as just "The Monument") is a 62 metre high stone column that stands near the spot where the fire started in 1666. You can climb to the top of the column for superb views over London. The view northeast to the City skyscrapers (pictured below) and southeast to Tower Bridge are particularly good. Access is via a narrow spiral staircase (there's no lift) and the top is covered by a mesh cage. If you have a compact camera you'll have no problem shooting through the holes in the mesh, however if you have an SLR with a lens wider than 6 cm then you're out of luck as the mesh will get in the way. Tripods are only allowed when it's quiet, but there is a wide flat railing you can rest your camera on for long exposures. The spiral staircase is also interesting to photograph.

» Practical Information

Tube: Monument

Bus: 17, 521, 21, 43, 133, 141, 48, 149

Web: www.themonument.info

Tel: 0207 626 2717

Open: April to September 9.30am – 6pm daily. October to March 9.30am – 5.30pm daily.

Closed: 24th–26th December, 1st January

Admission: £4 for adults, £2 for children

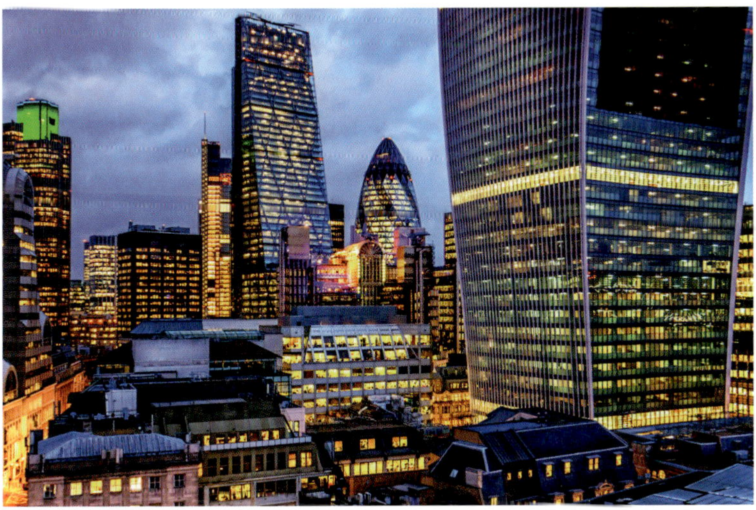

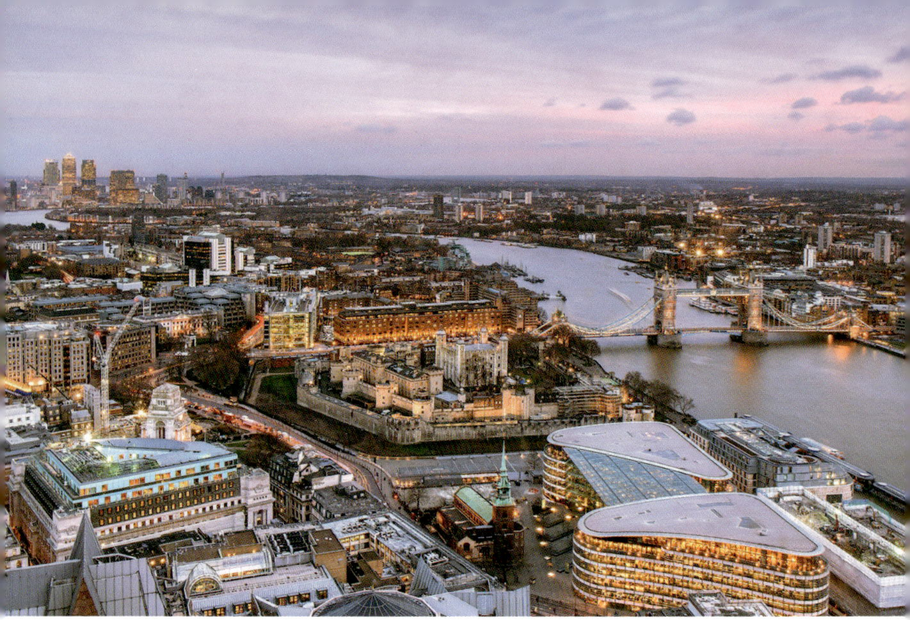

38 THE SKY GARDEN

At the top of 20 Fenchurch Street (also known as the "Walkie Talkie") there is a public garden called the Sky Garden. It has absolutely fabulous 360° views over London, with all the major landmarks visible, such as the Shard, St Paul's, the Gherkin and the Tower of London. To top it off it's completely free to visit, however you have to book tickets at least three days in advance through the website. Although there's an open–air terrace on the south side all the views are from behind glass, so reflections can be a problem. If you can't get a ticket for the date you want, the alternative is to book a table at one of the restaurants inside as diners have free access to the gardens. The entrance is on the southwest corner of the building on Philpot Lane and you have to pass through airport–style security and show photo ID to get in. N.B. tripods aren't allowed and if it's busy you may be limited to 1½ hours inside.

» Practical Information

Tube: Monument

Bus: 15, 40

Web: www.skygarden.london

Open: 10am – 6pm Monday to Friday, 11am – 9pm Saturday and Sunday.

Admission: Free

39 THE GHERKIN

This striking building is officially called 30 St Mary Axe but is widely know as "The Gherkin". It can be seen from many places in London but up close and personal it's great to photograph. One of the best locations to shoot it from is Leadenhall Street, next to the Lloyd's Building. From here you get a great view of the Gherkin nestled behind

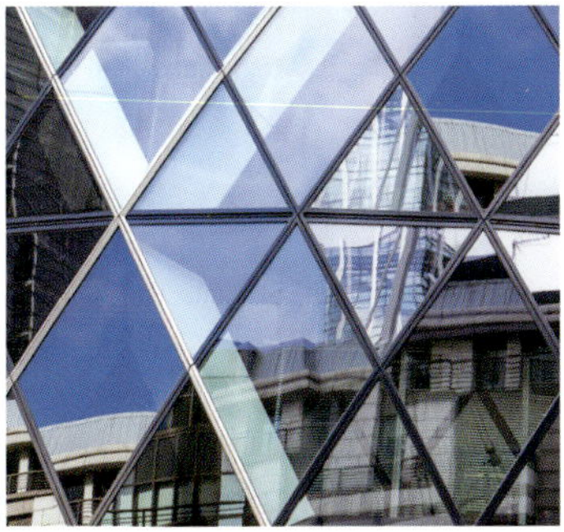

St Andrew Undershaft Church, creating a stark contrast between old and new (pictured below). There's plenty to explore from the base of the building too – the front entrance is interesting (especially at night) and you can get great detail shots of other buildings reflected in the glass panels (like the one pictured above). If you're after a photo of the top poking out above the rooftops then try Billiter Street or Fenchurch Buildings (both off Fenchurch Street – point 39A on the map).

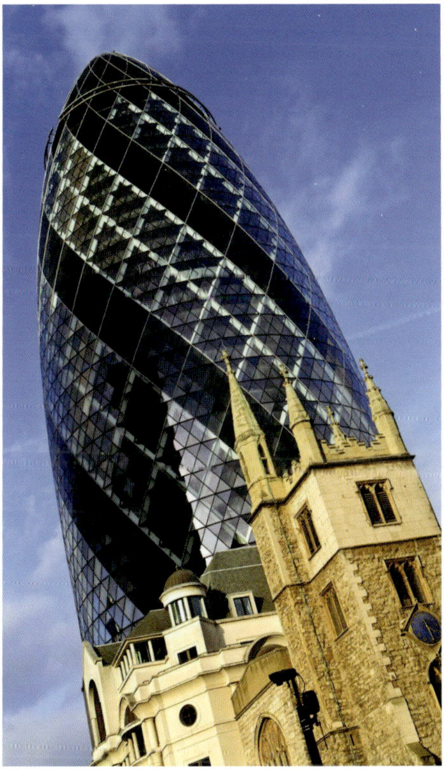

» Practical Information

Tube: Liverpool Street, Bank, Monument

Bus: 25, 35, 47, 48, 149, 344, N35, N550, N551

40 THE LLOYD'S BUILDING

This unusual modern building is home to the insurance giant Lloyd's of London. It's also known as the "inside-out building" because a lot of the service structures are on the exterior, such as the stairwells, lifts and pipework. It's tightly surrounded by other buildings so to take it all in you'll spend most of your time looking up. Make sure you go all the way around the base of the building to explore all the different angles. Close-ups of interesting sections of the building work well, as do compositions that also include neighbouring buildings, such as the Leadenhall Building or the curved front of the Willis Building (pictured below). There's also a good view from Lime Street, looking between the Lloyd's Building and the Willis Building to the Gherkin. It's wonderful to photograph at night as it's illuminated by lots of different coloured lights, although it's still a good location during the day, especially if you're lucky enough to have a blue sky.

» Practical Information

Tube: Monument, Bank, Liverpool Street

Bus: 25, 35, 47, 48, 149, 344, N35, N550, N551

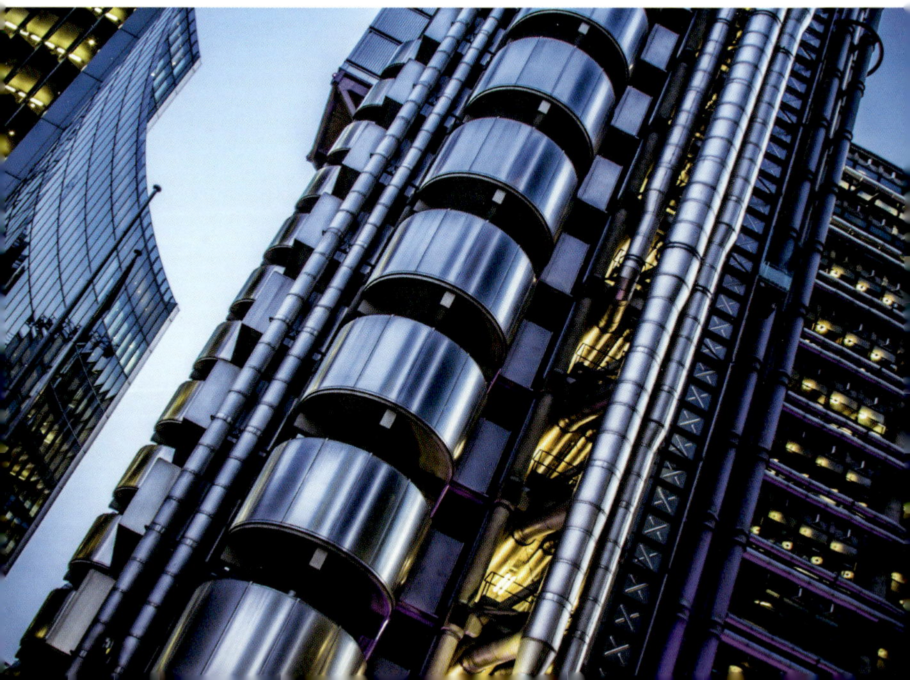

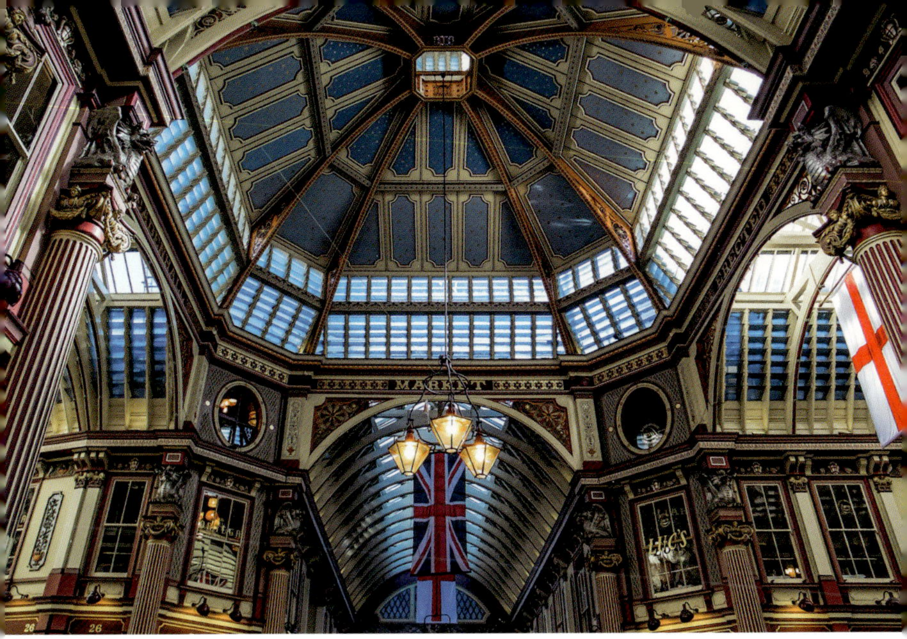

41 LEADENHALL MARKET

This historic Victorian marketplace is now essentially a shopping arcade rather than a traditional market, but it's still packed with character and interesting to photograph. The cobbled floors, old-fashioned shop fronts and beautiful arched glass roof create a really charming atmosphere. This is further added to by little details, such as gold gilding and lanterns hanging overhead. There are plenty of angles to explore here, although the most popular is to shoot from the centre looking out along a shop-lined passageway. Another interesting feature to photograph is the roof of the central area (pictured above), so don't forget to look up while you're in there. If you want to capture the market with the hustle and bustle of city life then go on a weekday around lunchtime. If you don't want people in your photos then go at the weekend when it's largely deserted, or at night after the shops have closed. It's particularly photogenic when decorated for Christmas.

» Practical Information

Tube: Monument, Bank
Bus: 25, 35, 47, 48, 149, 344, N35, N550
Open: You can walk through it at any time of day or night (the entrances aren't gated or locked), but the shops are only open on weekdays.

42 ST DUNSTAN IN THE EAST

This small parish church was unfortunately severely damaged during the Blitz in 1941. Only the walls and tower survived the bombing and eventually the ruins were turned into a public garden, which is an oasis of peacefulness amidst the hustle and bustle of the city. What makes it interesting to photograph is that over time various vines and other climbing plants have grown along the walls and through the delicate window frames, creating a rather charming atmosphere. This ambience is further added to by cobbled floors, arched doorways and wooden benches.

The best times of year to visit are during summer when the plants are at their most verdant, and in autumn when you'll find an array of beautiful golden colours.

» Practical Information

Directions: The church is just off St Dunstan's Hill, between Lower Thames Street and Great Tower Street.

Tube: Monument, Tower Hill

Bus: 15, N15

Pier: Tower

Open: Every day 8am – 7pm or dusk (whichever is earlier)

Access: There's step–free access to the top part of the garden on Idol Lane.

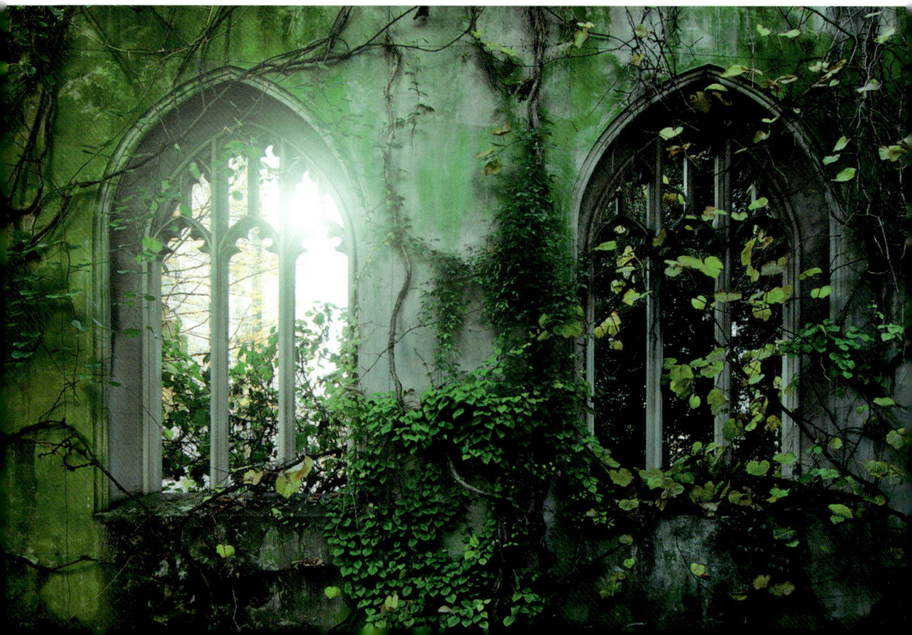

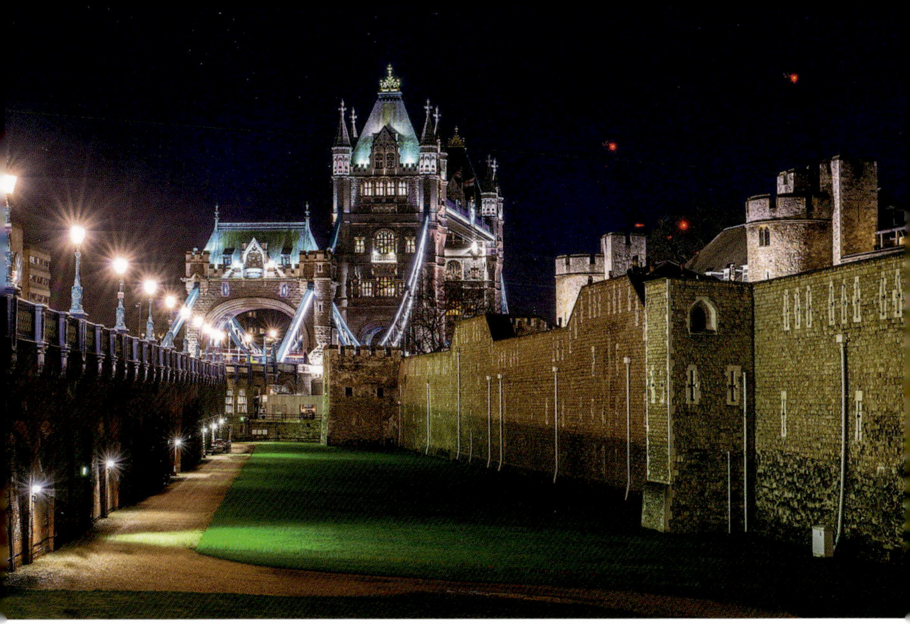

43 THE TOWER OF LONDON

The Tower of London is one of the most famous buildings in London, but it's surprisingly difficult to get a really good photograph of it. You can walk all the way around the outer walls at any time of day or night, so my best advice would be to circle it to find an angle you like. Saying that, the view from the northeastern corner that also includes Tower Bridge is particularly good – pictured above (43A on the map). Another good viewpoint is from the southern bank of the Thames, next to City Hall. From here you get the best view of the White Tower in the middle and it's a great spot to photograph it at night. If you have your heart set on a photo of a Beefeater (tower guard) you may catch sight of one at the entrance gates, but the only way to guarantee getting a photo of them is to pay to go inside, where they conduct guided tours.

» Practical Information

Tube: Tower Hill

Bus: 15, 42, 78, 100, RV1

Pier: Tower, St Katherine's

Web: www.hrp.org.uk/TowerOfLondon

Tel: 0844 482 7777

Open: March to October 9am – 5.30pm. November to February 9am – 4.30pm.

Closed: 24th–26th December, January 1st

Admission: Adult £25, child £11

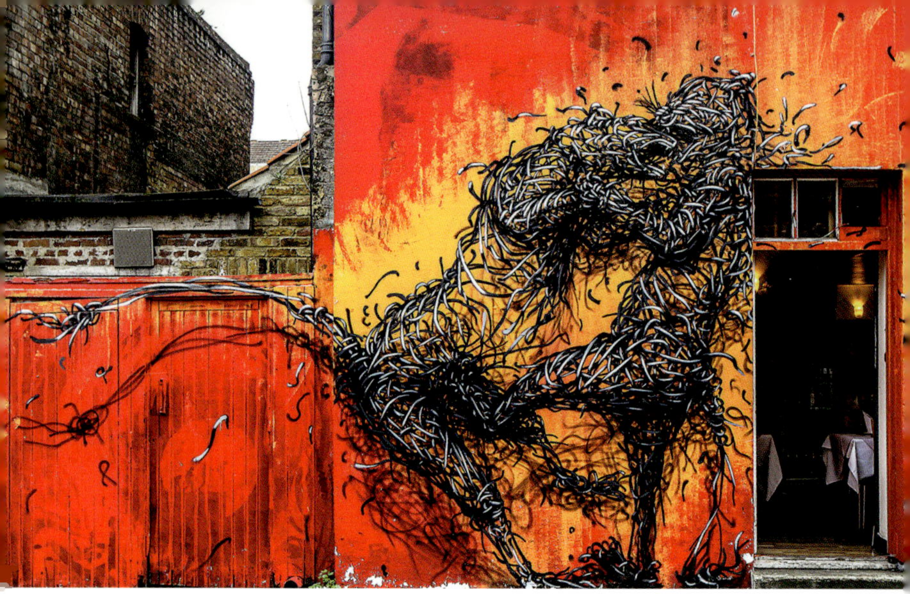

44 BRICK LANE

This street is the heart of London's Bangladeshi community and is a good location for photography for two reasons – the Sunday market and the street art that adorns the walls in various places. You'll find the market at the northern end of the street, where it also spills into some of the side streets. It offers everything from food and furniture to second-hand books and bric-a-brac. It's a lot more chaotic than other London markets, which makes it all the more interesting, and there are also plenty of opportunities for street photography. The street art constantly changes, so you don't know what you might find or where – my advice is to walk the full length of the street (it's not that long) and keep your eye out for interesting pieces. It's also worth looking along the side streets, particularly Hanbury Street, Pedley Street and Sclater Street, and down any little alleys you find, such as the one between Fashion Street and Fournier Street.

» Practical Information

Tube: Aldgate East, Aldgate, Liverpool Street

Train: Shoreditch High Street, Liverpool Street

Bus: 8, 26, 35, 43 (Sunday market hours only), 47, 48, 67, 78, 149, 242

Web: www.visitbricklane.org

Open: The market is only on Sundays 9am – 5pm.

45 COLUMBIA ROAD FLOWER MARKET

Every Sunday on Columbia Road the street is filled with stalls selling everything from bulbs and shrubs to house plants and cut flowers. What's on offer varies with the seasons, but you'll always find a bewildering array of greenery and a huge spectrum of colours. Try capturing the bustle of the market and the lively traders in action, or focus in on attractive displays or even individual flowers. (If you want to include the traders in a photograph, be polite and ask them if it's OK first.) Also, there are plenty of opportunities for street photography, as there are often buskers playing music in the street and there are always people milling around the trendy gift shops and cafes that are dotted along the road. It can get very busy around lunchtime, so if you prefer it quieter go early.

» Practical Information

Tube: Bethnal Green, Old Street

Train: Hoxton, Shoreditch High Street

Bus: 26, 48, 55, 8, 388

Web: www.columbiaroad.info

Open: Sundays only, from 8am to about 3pm

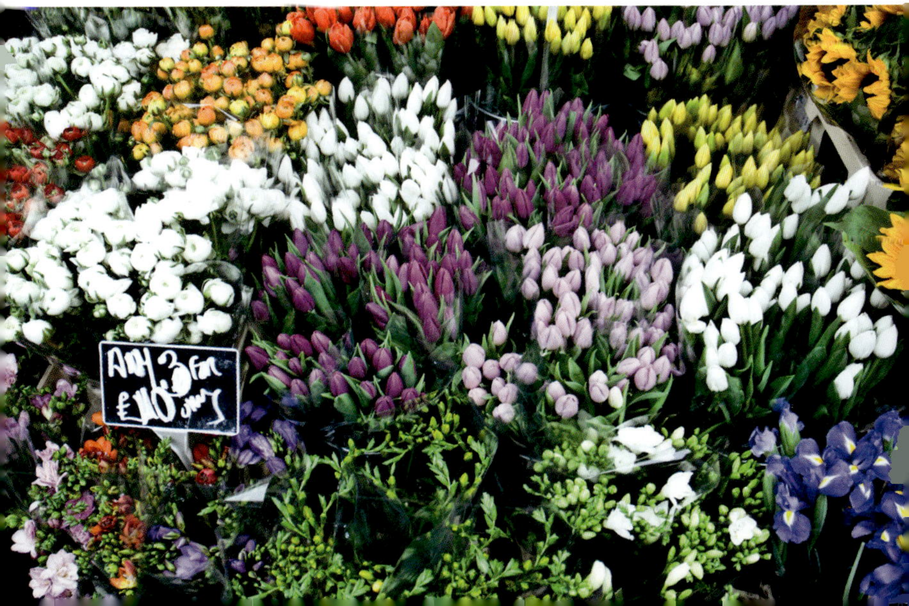

6 SECTION Docklands & Greenwich

The docklands area is in east London and spans many different London boroughs. It was once the heart of London's shipping industry, but eventually the docks closed as new ports nearer the coast became more practical. Canary Wharf was created as part of their redevelopment and is now one of the major financial centres in the world. It contains some of the tallest buildings in London and is built around the West India Docks, which is made up of many small docks. There's lots to photograph in the area, from skyscrapers to tube stations, although it really comes into its own at night when the buildings are lit up and reflected in the water. I'd recommend visiting at the weekend when it's much quieter, although at night any day of the week is fine. Another photogenic area in the docklands is the Royal Victoria Dock. This is much less visited than other areas but has some good photo opportunities.

To the south of Canary Wharf is Greenwich, which has a rich maritime history and is a World Heritage Site. It has a lovely small–town feel and some beautiful Georgian and Victorian architecture. There's a variety of subjects to photograph here, such as the Greenwich Foot Tunnel and views from Greenwich Park. The Old Royal Naval College is a must–visit location, with superb exterior and interior architecture. Also not to miss is the stunning spiral staircase at the Queen's House.

On the Greenwich Peninsula to the east of Greenwich town lies the O2 Arena, which is a major entertainment venue. It's a striking building with a domed roof and supporting poles jutting out. This can be photographed from ground level near Canary Wharf or from above on the Emirates Cable Car, which runs across the Thames to Royal Victoria Dock.

Moving further east again you'll find the Thames Barrier. This is one of the largest movable flood barriers in the world and was built to protect over 50 square miles of central London from being flooded by high tides and storm surges. Although it's not as easy to get to as some of the other locations it's well worth a visit, especially for sunset.

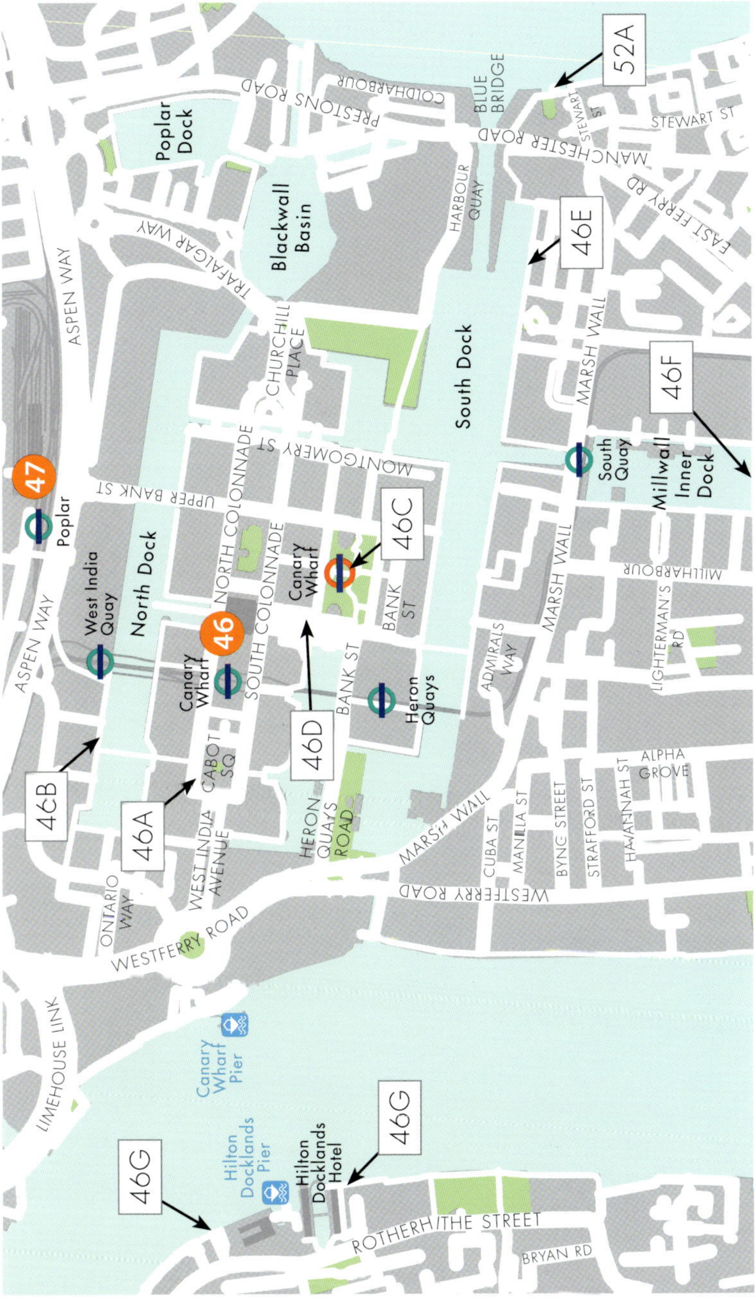

52A
46E
46F
46C
46D
46B
46A
46G
46G
46
47
Poplar Dock
Blackwall Basin
South Dock
North Dock
Millwall Inner Dock
Poplar
West India Quay
Canary Wharf
Canary Wharf
Heron Quays
South Quay
Canary Wharf Pier
Hilton Docklands Pier
Hilton Docklands Hotel
PRESTONS ROAD
COLDHARBOUR
BLUE BRIDGE
MANCHESTER ROAD
STEWART ST
STEWART ST
EAST FERRY RD
HARBOUR QUAY
TRAFALGAR WAY
ASPEN WAY
ASPEN WAY
CHURCHILL PLACE
MONTGOMERY ST
UPPER BANK ST
NORTH COLONNADE
SOUTH COLONNADE
BANK ST
BANK ST
MARSH WALL
MARSH WALL
MARSH WALL
MILLHARBOUR
LIGHTERMAN'S RD
ADMIRALS WAY
CABOT SQ
WEST INDIA AVENUE
HERON QUAYS ROAD
ONTARIO WAY
WESTFERRY ROAD
WESTFERRY ROAD
CUBA ST
MANILLA ST
BYNG STREET
STRAFFORD ST
HAVANNAH ST
ALPHA GROVE
LIMEHOUSE LINK
ROTHERHITHE STREET
BRYAN RD

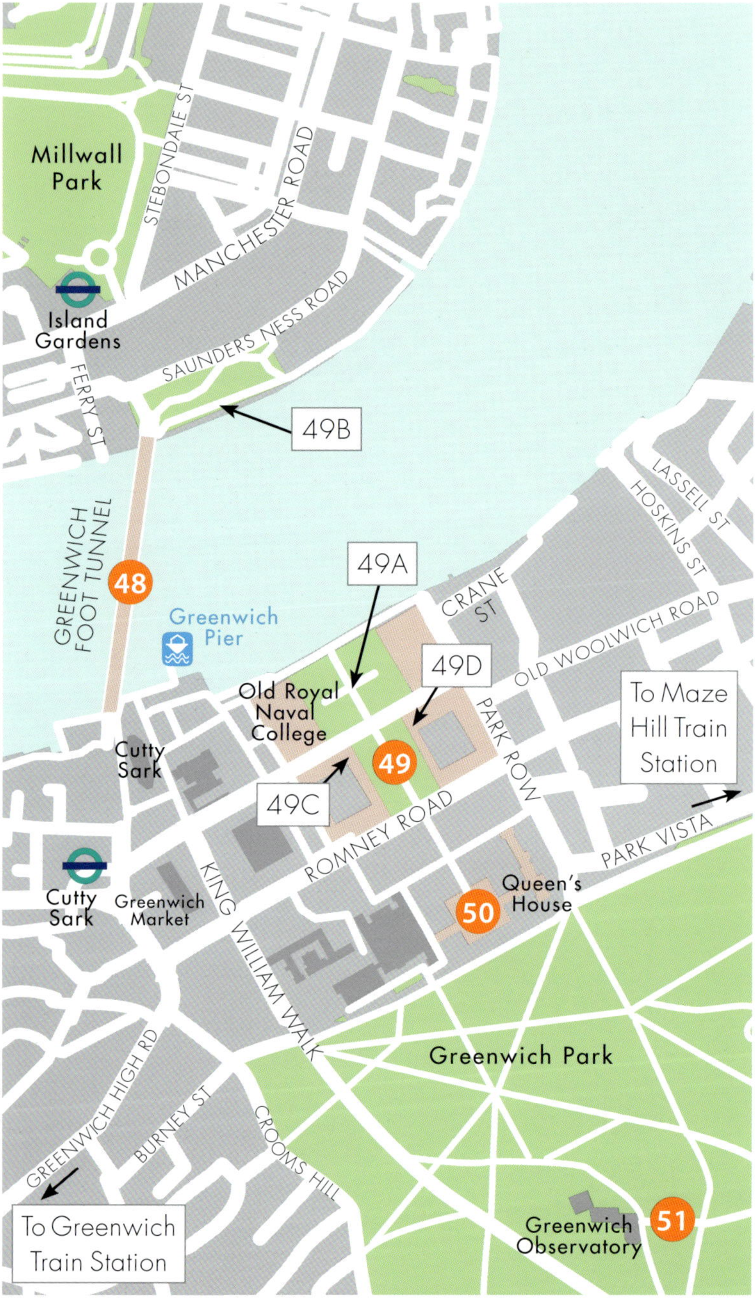

Millwall Park
STEBONDALE ST
MANCHESTER ROAD
Island Gardens
SAUNDERS NESS ROAD
FERRY ST
49B
GREENWICH FOOT TUNNEL
48
Greenwich Pier
49A
CRANE ST
LASSELL ST
HOSKINS ST
OLD WOOLWICH ROAD
49D
Old Royal Naval College
PARK ROW
To Maze Hill Train Station
Cutty Sark
49
49C
ROMNEY ROAD
PARK VISTA
KING WILLIAM WALK
Cutty Sark
Greenwich Market
Queen's House
50
Greenwich Park
GREENWICH HIGH RD
BURNEY ST
CROOMS HILL
To Greenwich Train Station
Greenwich Observatory
51

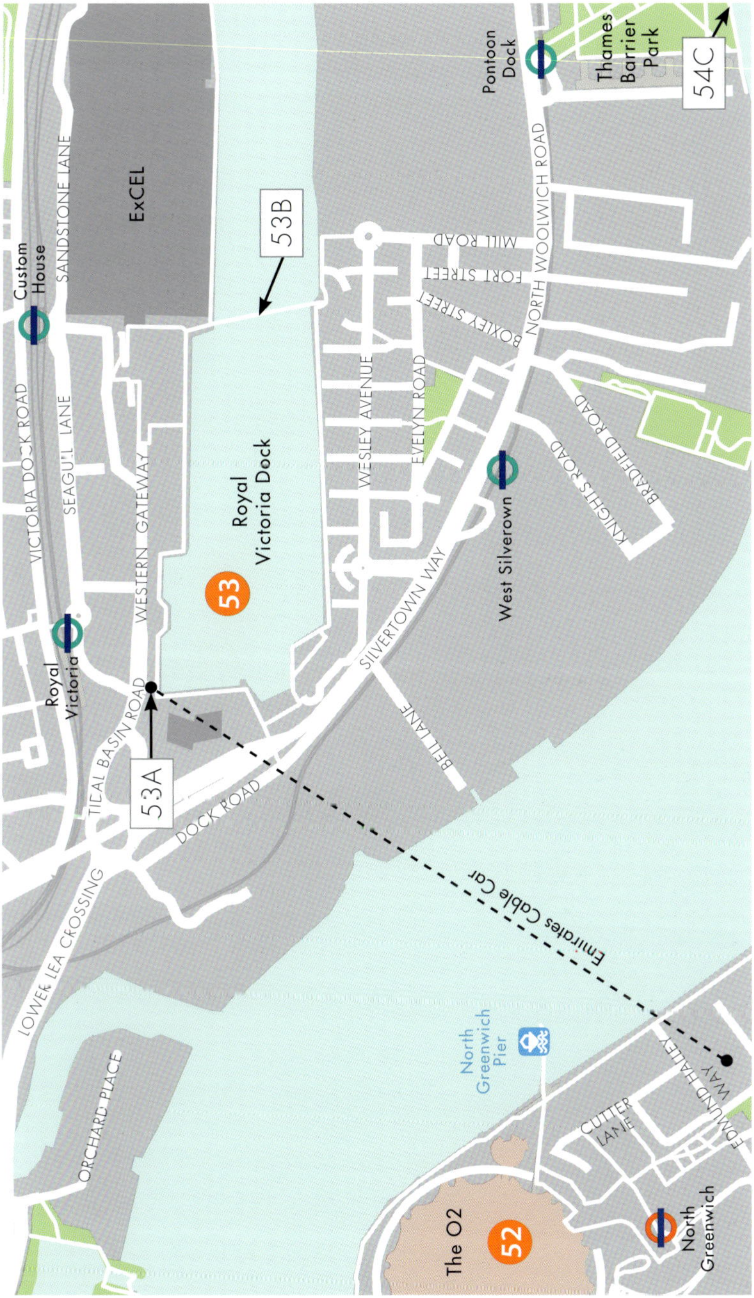

ExCEL
Custom House
Royal Victoria
Royal Victoria Dock
53
53A
53B
54C
West Silverown
Pontoon Dock
Thames Barrier Park
The O2
52
North Greenwich
North Greenwich Pier
Emirates Cable Car
VICTORIA DOCK ROAD
SANDSTONE LANE
SEAGULL LANE
WESTERN GATEWAY
TIDAL BASIN ROAD
DOCK ROAD
LOWER LEA CROSSING
SILVERTOWN WAY
WESLEY AVENUE
EVELYN ROAD
BOXLEY STREET
FORT STREET
MILL ROAD
NORTH WOOLWICH ROAD
KNIGHTS ROAD
BRADFIELD ROAD
BELL LANE
ORCHARD PLACE
CUTTER LANE
EDMUND HALLEY WAY

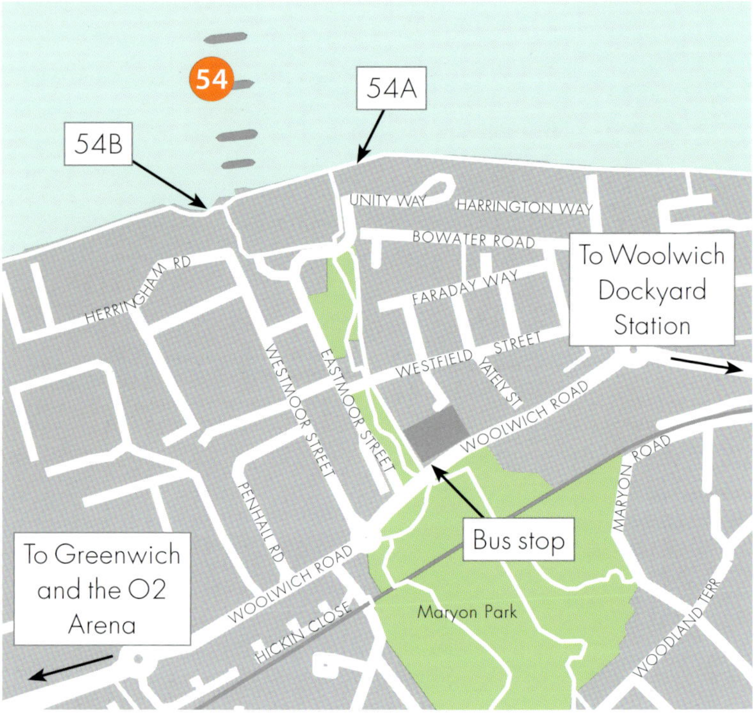

46 CANARY WHARF

There's so much to photograph at Canary Wharf you could easily spend a whole day there, but it's most photogenic at night-time when all the buildings are lit up.

The first location I'd recommend is Cabot Square – point 46A on the map. From here you get an great view of the imposing One Canada Square building (the tallest one with the pyramidal roof). The surrounding buildings frame the scene nicely and the fountain in the square makes excellent foreground.

Just to the north of the square by the bridge over the North Dock is another good viewpoint (point 46B on the map). A popular angle to shoot is southwest, with the bridge and the buildings reflected in the water. Alternatively, stand on the northern end of the bridge and shoot along it, using the railings to lead the eye to the buildings behind (if you're using a tripod beware of vibrations on the bridge).

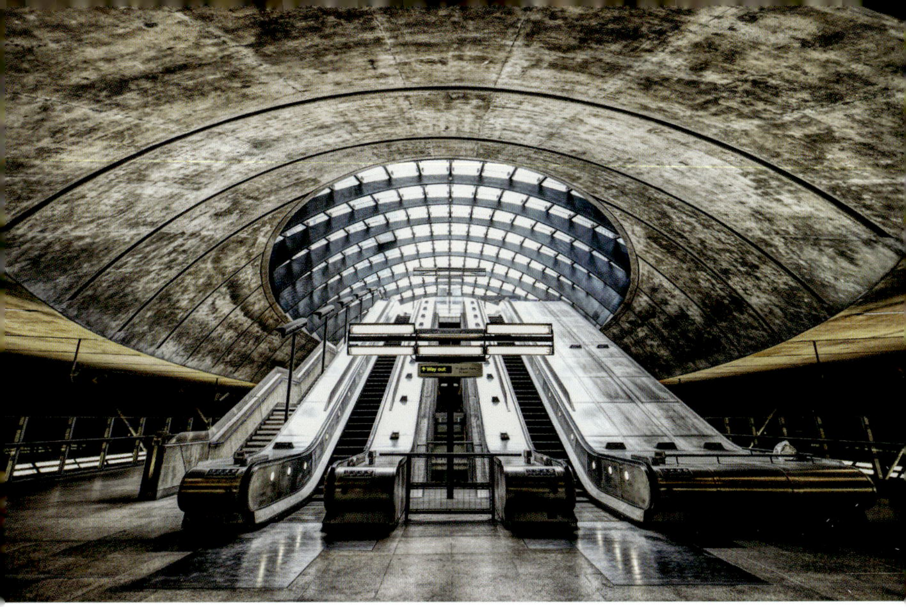

At the heart of Canary Wharf is the underground station (point 46C on the map). The curved glass canopies that cover the entrances are interesting to photograph, especially the small entrance in Montgomery Square as it has wiggly paving in front of it that makes great leading lines. However, the star attraction of the station are the escalators inside at the west and east entrances. They look fabulous shot from the bottom looking up to the glass canopy (pictured above). This is one location at Canary Wharf that's best photographed during the day as it can be quite dark inside and tripods aren't allowed. See p105 for important info about taking photos in tube stations.

Near the tube station is Reuters Plaza, where you'll find an art installation of clocks on tall posts (point 46D on the map). These look great isolated against a skyscraper such as One Canada Square – pictured below. Long exposure shots of people walking through them also work really well. A good

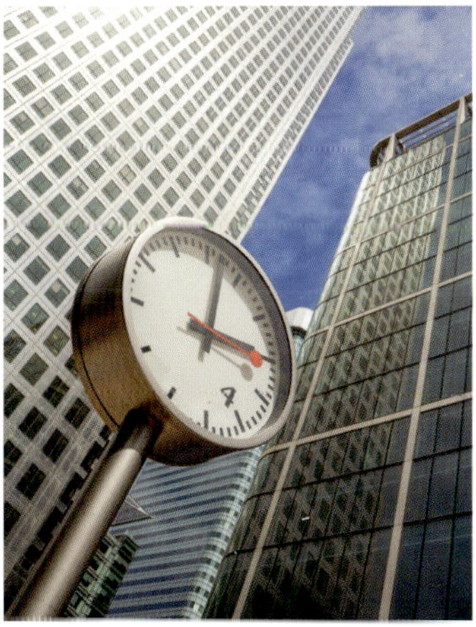

vantage point for this is above the shopping centre entrance, looking down on the plaza.

For the best view of the skyline head for the eastern corner of the South Dock (pictured below – point 46E on the map). There are often some boats moored down at this end of the dock, which you can include in your composition, and as you'd expect it's best when the wind is low so you get good reflections. It's a suitable location for sunrise as the warm morning sun hits the buildings and also for sunset as you're looking roughly west.

If you don't mind stretching your legs a bit there's another superb skyscraper view at Millwall Inner Dock (point 46F on the map). From the bridge at the bottom end you get a great composition looking north, with the floating Lotus restaurant on the right and the buildings reflected in the water.

A final location I'd recommend for capturing the skyline is from the banks of the Thames at Rotherhithe, to the west of Canary Wharf (points 46G on the map). The waterfront is accessible either side of the Hilton Docklands Hotel and has an uninterrupted view across to Canary Wharf. There's also an unusual shot looking over the old dock between the Hilton buildings. The buildings frame the skyscrapers perfectly and a footbridge running over the water adds interest to the scene.

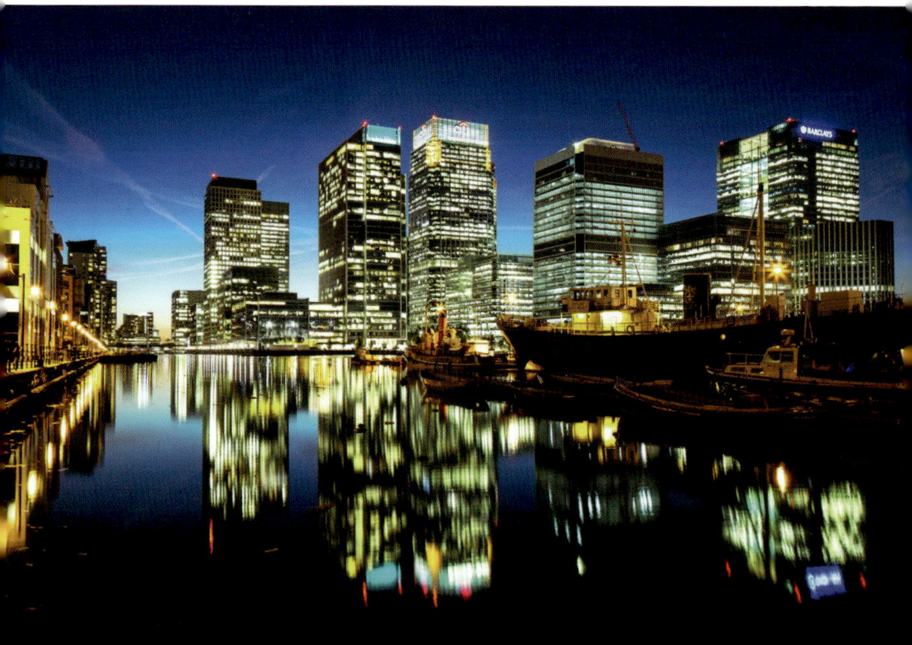

» Practical Information

Tube: Canary Wharf

DLR: Canary Wharf

Pier: Canary Wharf

Bus: D3, D7, D8, 135, 277, N550

For Rotherhithe: Use the Canada Water tube station, Rotherhithe train station, the C10 bus or take the ferry from Canary Wharf Pier to the Hilton Docklands Pier.

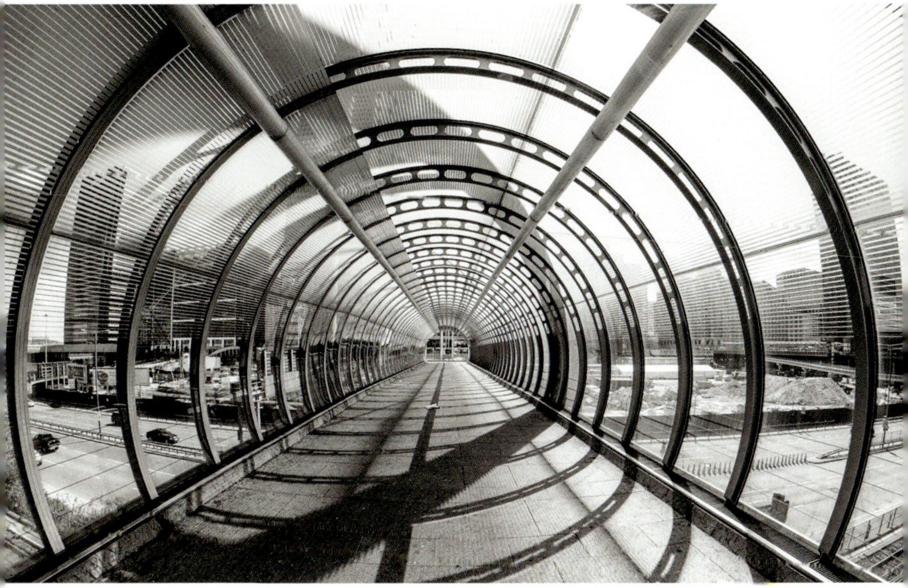

47 POPLAR DLR BRIDGE

At the Poplar DLR Station is a cylindrical footbridge that goes over the railway tracks. It's one of those odd places that isn't very picturesque but is strangely photogenic (you could easily walk across it without giving it a second thought, but get your camera out and it's a different matter). The best time to visit it is on a sunny day, as the curved metalwork casts interesting shadows on the floor. N.B. tripods aren't allowed.

» Practical Information

The easiest way to get there is to take the DLR. From the platform just follow the exit signs up the stairs to the bridge.

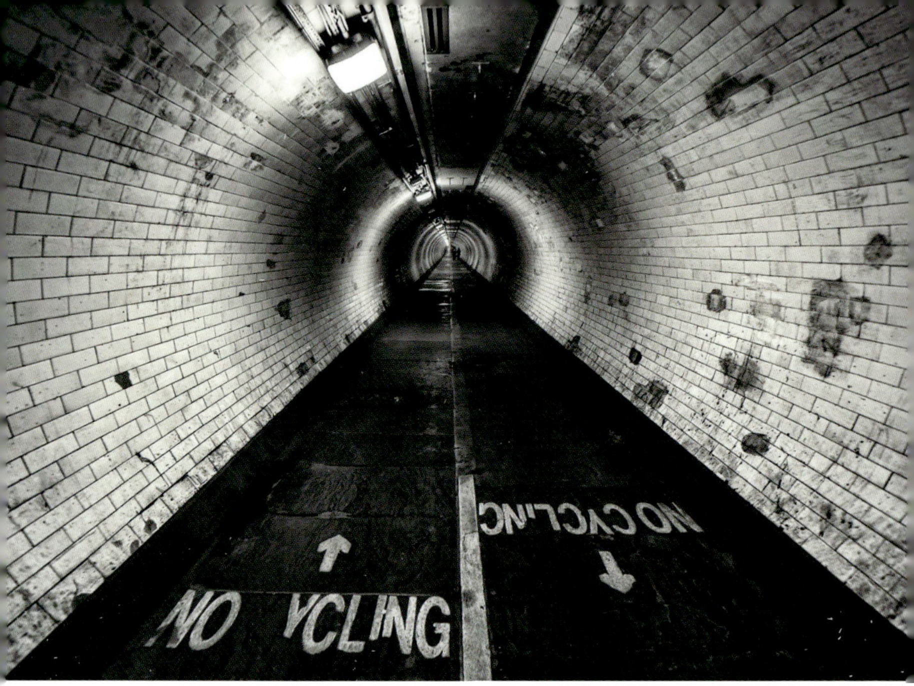

48 GREENWICH FOOT TUNNEL

This tunnel stretches nearly 400 metres under the River Thames, linking Greenwich with the Isle of Dogs to the north. The tunnel is lined with tiles and has a slightly grimy feel, but makes a very interesting photograph as the lines converge in the distance (pictured above). Make sure you explore the northern end of the tunnel too, as there's a narrower section that was damaged during World War II and is now reinforced with steel cladding. As you may have guessed it's pretty dark in the tunnel so a tripod is recommended.

The circular tunnel entrances at each end are covered by glazed domes and also make interesting photographic subjects, especially at night. The southern entrance at Greenwich is particularly photogenic, as you can include the skyscrapers of Canary Wharf in the background (pictured top right). It's also right next to the Cutty Sark – a historic clipper ship that's now a museum and is encased in a glass housing to preserve it. It can be included in a composition of the tunnel entrance or shot on its own – a favoured composition is from the bow (pictured bottom right).

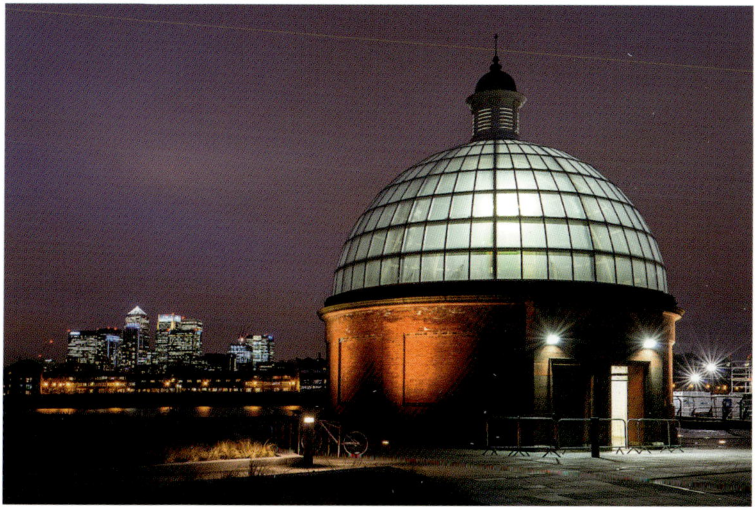

» Practical Information

DLR: Cutty Sark, Island Gardens

Train: Greenwich, Maze Hill

Pier: Greenwich

Bus: 129, 177, 180, 188, 199, 286, 386

Open: 24 hours a day (access for wheelchairs via lifts at either end)

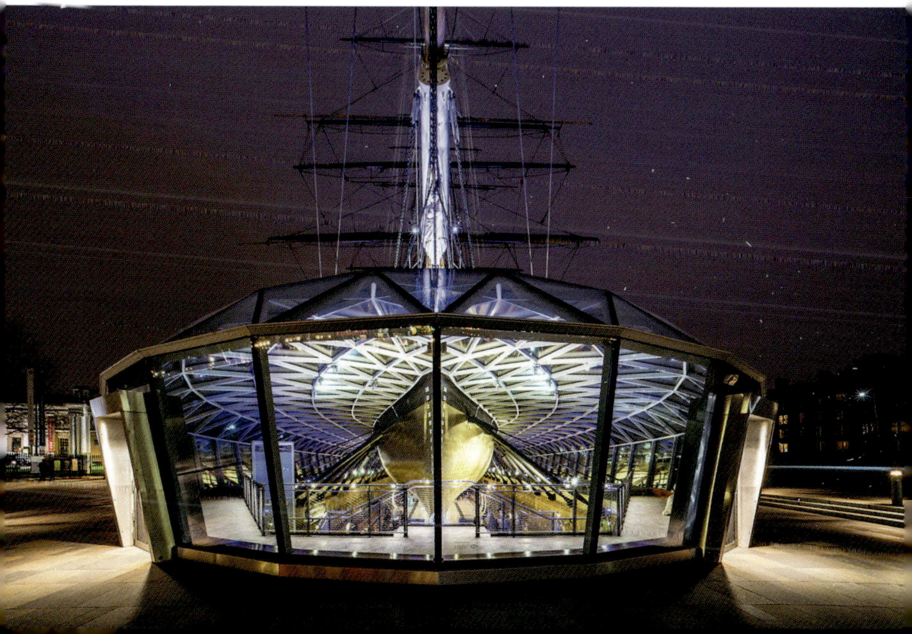

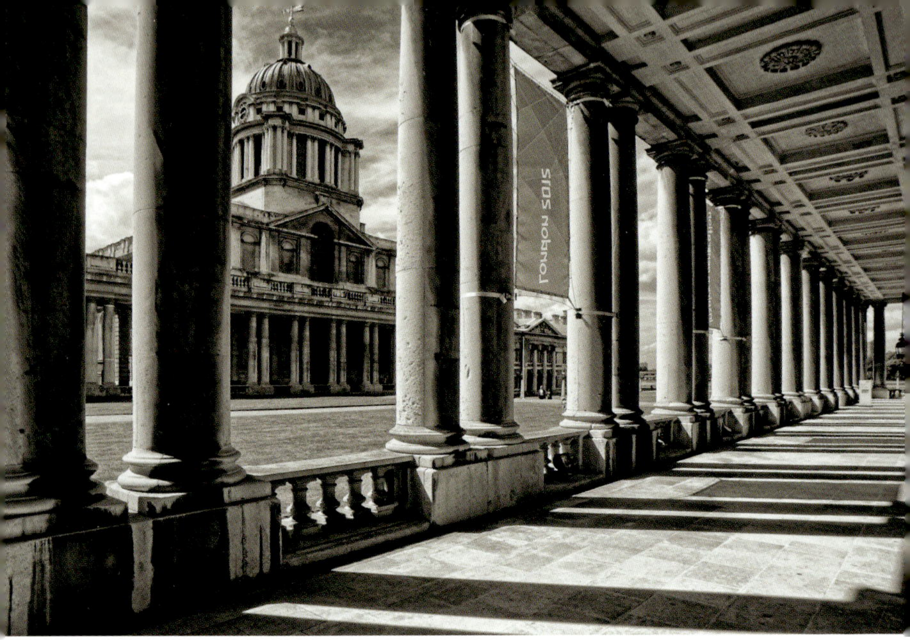

49 OLD ROYAL NAVAL COLLEGE

The Old Royal Naval College is packed with subjects to photograph. The beautiful baroque buildings alone could occupy any photographer for a good while, especially the colonnades (pictured above). There's a great view of the buildings from the George II statue near the Thames (point 49A on the map), where you can use the paved path as a leading line to the twin domes. To get a wider view try from the north bank of the Thames, just beside the entrance to Greenwich Foot Tunnel (point 49B on the map).

Inside one of the domed buildings you'll find the Painted Hall (pictured bottom right – point 49C on the map). This is one of the finest dining halls in Europe and as you'd expect from the name it's elaborately painted. If you study the walls and ceilings you'll find everything from famous astronomers to signs of the zodiac and characters from Greek mythology. There are small mirrored tables in the hall to help you view the ceiling, but they can also be used for some unusual compositions. Also, don't miss the ceiling of the entrance hall as it's particularly photogenic.

In the other domed building you'll find the Chapel, which is neoclassical in style and also ornately decorated (pictured top right – point 49D on the map). The classic shot of this is from the entrance looking down the pews towards the altar, but there are also lots of subjects for close-up detail shots, such as the organ, the huge altarpiece painting and the intricate blue and cream plaster ceiling. N.B. tripods aren't allowed anywhere on the site.

» Practical Information

DLR: Cutty Sark

Train: Greenwich, Maze Hill

Pier: Greenwich

Bus: 129, 177, 180, 188, 199, 286, 386

Open: 8am – 11pm for the grounds, 10am – 5pm for the Painted Hall & Chapel

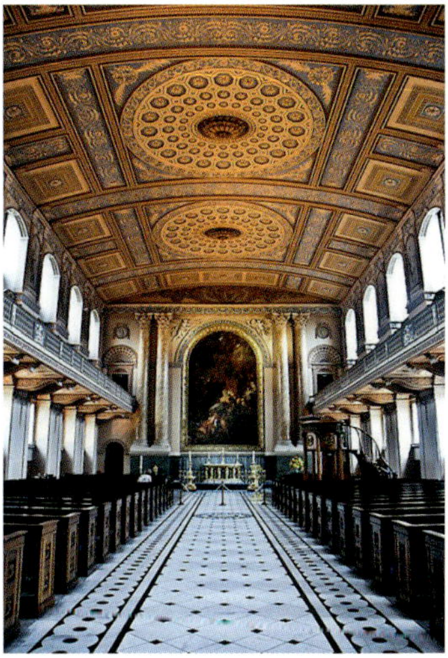

Closed: 24th – 26th December

Web: www.ornc.org

Tel: 020 8269 4747

Admission: Free

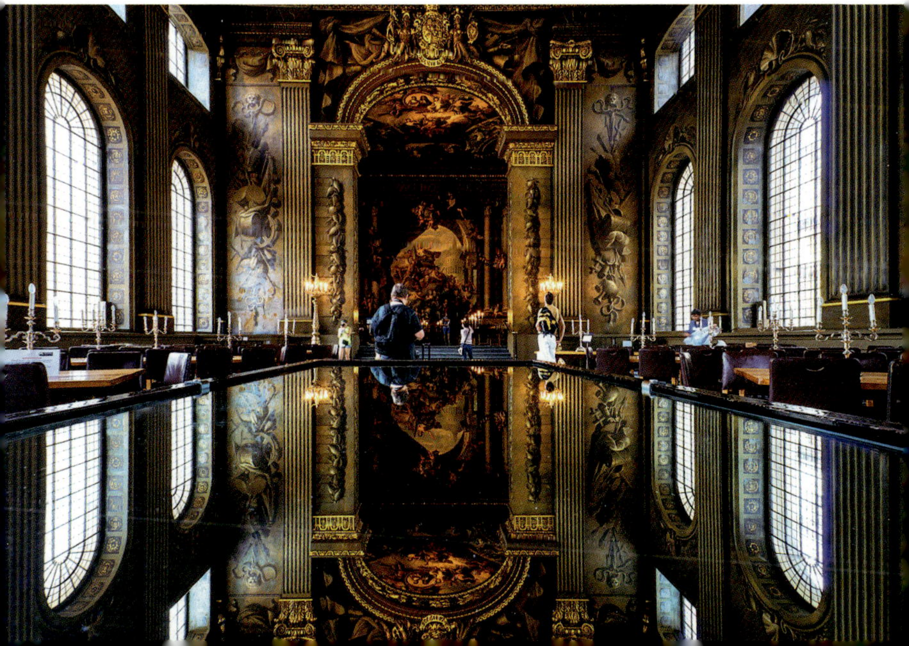

50 THE TULIP STAIRS

The Queen's House at Greenwich is a former royal residence built in the 1600s. Inside you'll find an elegant staircase called the Tulip Stairs (named after the floral design of the handrail, although the flowers are in fact fleur-de-lis not tulips). It was designed by Inigo Jones and was the first self-supporting helical staircase in England. It's best shot from the bottom looking upwards (pictured on the right) and there's plenty of space at the foot of the staircase to explore different compositions. The contrast between the stairs and the ironwork of the railings means it also works particularly well in black and white. While you're in the building make sure you have a look at the Great Hall as well, which has an interesting black and white patterned marble floor. Also, outside the Queen's House there are two beautiful colonnades that link the house to nearby buildings. These look great on a bright day when the columns cast strong shadows onto the paved stone floor.

» Practical Information

DLR: Cutty Sark

Pier: Greenwich

Train: Maze Hill

Bus: 129, 177, 180, 188, 199, 286, 386

Web: www.rmg.co.uk

Tel: 020 8858 4422

Open: 10am – 5pm every day

Closed: 24th – 26th December (plus occasional closures for private events – check the website for details).

Admission: Free

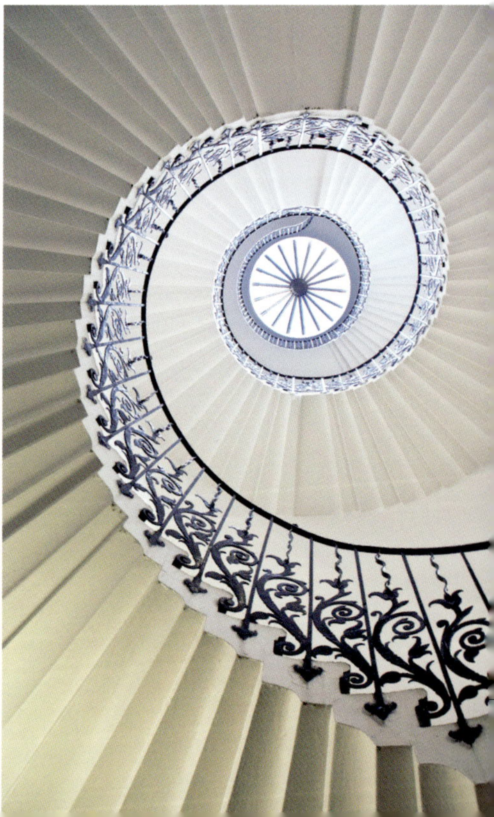

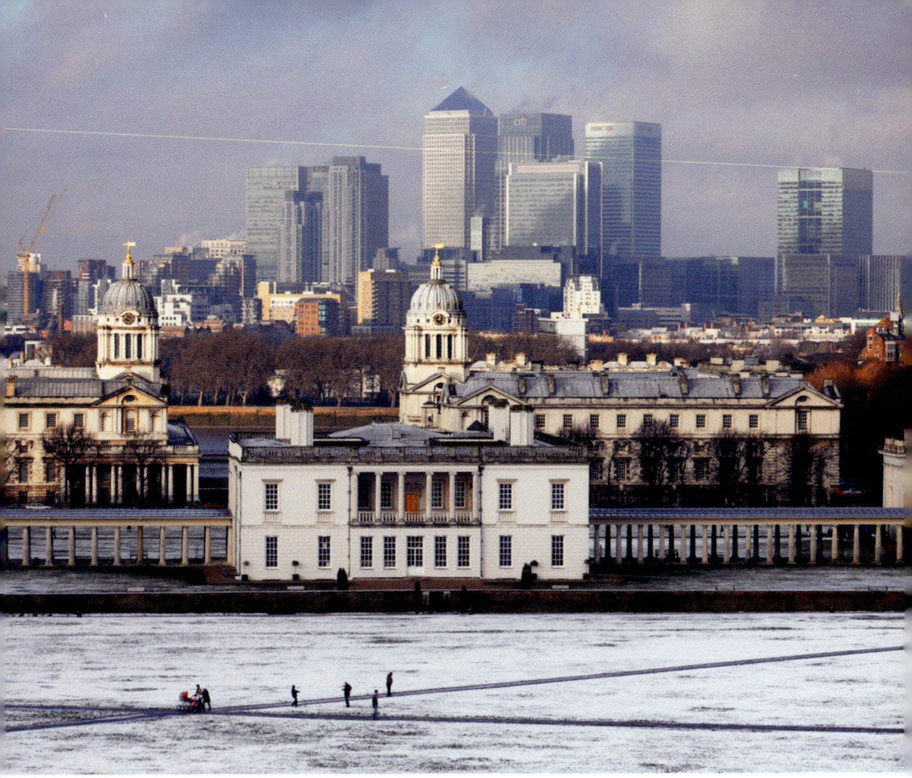

51 GREENWICH PARK

This is one of the many Royal Parks in London and covers around 180 acres. At the top of the hill sits the Royal Observatory and from the viewpoint next to it you get a fabulous panorama over Greenwich and beyond. To the west you can see the skyscrapers of the City and to the east the 02 Arena and Greenwich Power Station. The best view however is looking directly north over the National Maritime Museum and Royal Naval College, with Canary Wharf in the background (pictured above). It's suitable for both sunrise and sunset, but is also great at night.

» Practical Information

DLR. Cutty Sark

Pier: Greenwich

Train: Maze Hill

Bus: 129, 177, 180, 188, 199, 286, 386

Open: The park opens at 6am every day and closes at 6pm in winter, 7 or 8pm in spring and autumn, and 9 or 9.30pm in summer.

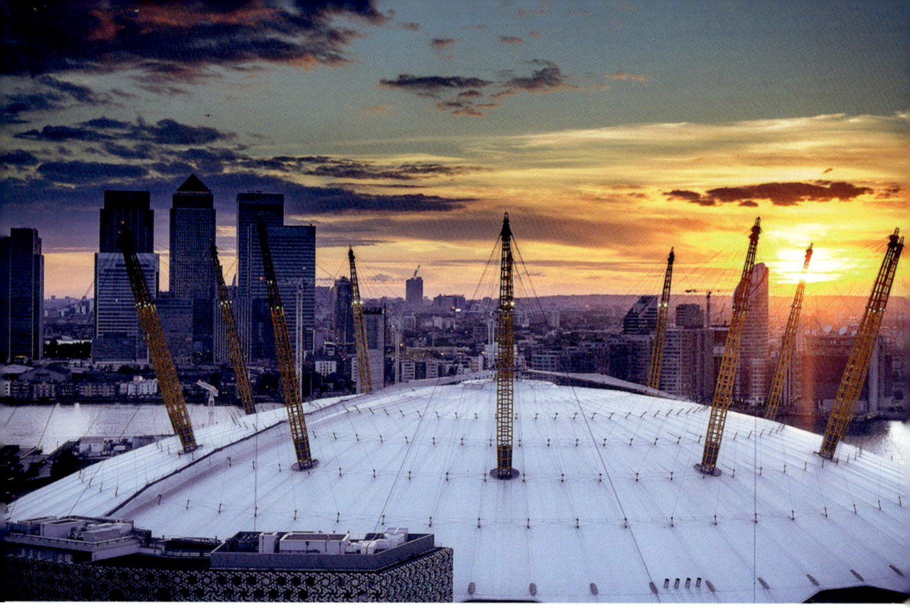

52 THE O2 ARENA

This huge structure was built to commemorate the millennium and is now a multi–purpose venue that hosts everything from concerts to sports events. A great place to capture it from is the Emirates Air Line cable car, which runs from The O2 over the Thames to Royal Victoria Dock. It takes you up to a height of 90 metres where you get a fabulous view of the arena with Canary Wharf in the background (pictured above). The crossing takes about 10 minutes and is best at sunset.

Another good location is on the banks of the Thames to the west of the arena (near Canary Wharf – point 52A on the map on page 82). From here you have an uninterrupted view of it across the river, which is best at sunrise or at night. Ideally, aim to visit in still conditions, as reflections of the dome and supporting masts in the water really improve the scene.

» Practical Information

Tube: North Greenwich

Pier: North Greenwich

Bus: 108, 129, 161, 188, 472

Emirates Air Line: It opens at 7am on weekdays, 8am on Saturdays and 9am on Sundays. It closes at 9pm in the summer (April to September) and 8pm in the winter (October to March). A single trip costs £4.50 for adults and £2.30 for children.

53 ROYAL VICTORIA DOCK

There are various points of photographic interest on this large dock and the best time to visit is at night when the wind is low and the surrounding buildings are reflected in the water.

Nestled in the northwestern corner of the dock is the cable car station for the Emirates Air Line, which looks superb when lit up at night (pictured below – point 53A on the map). Even with a bit of wind you have a decent chance of still water and good reflections here as there's a small pontoon cordoning off the corner it's in. Nearby is a building called the Crystal, which is mainly glass so also looks great photographed at night. Also, lining the quayside you'll find huge old cranes that were once used to load cargo onto ships. These add to the industrial feel of the dock, but also add interest to any composition.

Midway along the dock is an extremely tall footbridge, built to allow ships to pass underneath (point 53B on the map). From the bridge you get a wide view over the dock and if you zoom in you get a good view of Canary Wharf too. As you're looking west it makes a perfect location for sunset. (If you're using a tripod on the bridge beware of

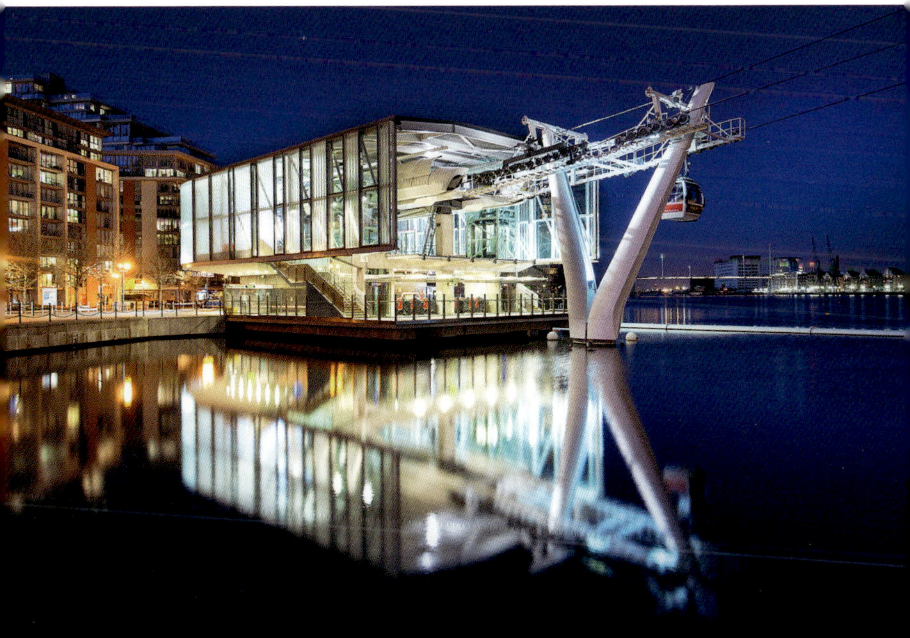

vibrations from people walking past). There's also an unusual composition of the bridge from directly underneath the southern end, looking across to the buildings on the northern side.

» Practical Information

DLR: Royal Victoria

Access: The bridge is accessible by stairs or lift, but the lifts are only open from 8am – 8pm.

54 THE THAMES BARRIER

The Thames Barrier was built in 1982 to protect London from tidal flooding. Across the 500 metre span of river there are seven huge stainless steel structures that raise the flood gates when needed. The best views of it are from the southern bank of the Thames. The first is from the eastern side of the barrier, looking west past the barrier with Canary Wharf and the O2 Arena in the background (pictured below – point 54A on the map). This view is particularly good at sunset. The other good viewpoint is from the western side of the barrier, looking north along the structure (pictured on the right – point 54B on the map). It's particularly good on a sunny

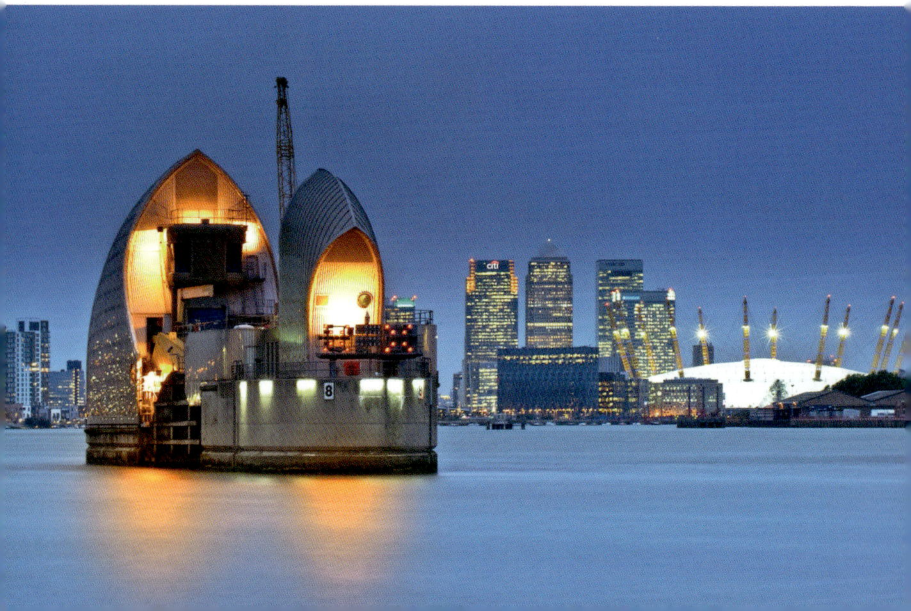

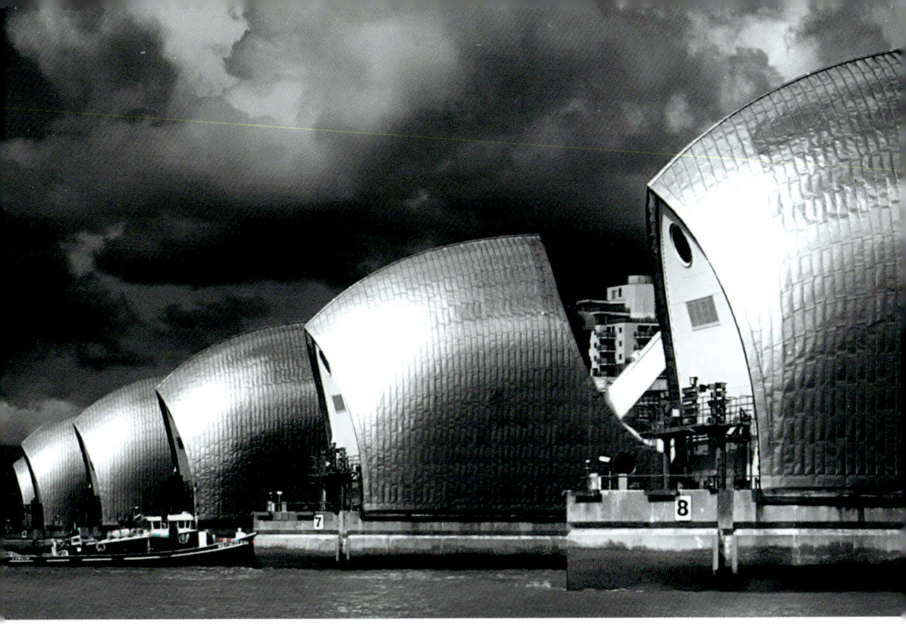

day, but both locations are also great at night.

If you just want to photograph the view along the barrier you can also do this from the northern bank of the Thames (point 54C on the map on page 84).

» Practical Information

Unfortunately, it's not easy to get to the southern side of the barrier. There's no tube station nearby and the nearest train station (Woolwich Dockyard) is a considerable walk away. In summer some river boats sail to the barrier, but don't actually stop at the pier. The easiest way to get there is to make your way to Greenwich or the O2 Arena and take a bus from there (number 177 or 180 from Greenwich, number 472 from the O2). Get off at the Royal Greenwich Uni Tech College bus stop then walk down Eastmoor Street. The bus ride can take anywhere between 10 and 30 minutes depending on the traffic, but the bus stops are announced so you know when yours is approaching. It's about a five minute walk from the bus stop to the barrier, where you'll find a small visitor centre and cafe. If you go at night don't be surprised if you're the only one there, which can be a bit eerie (both the river front and Eastmoor Street have street lights though).

To get to the viewpoint on the northern bank of the Thames, take the DLR to Pontoon Dock and walk through the Thames Barrier Park to the waterfront.

Extra Locations

Tube Stations

There are photo opportunities in pretty much every tube station in London, but as well as the ones listed in the main part of the book (Baker Street, Southwark and Canary Wharf) there are a few more that are particularly good for photography:

London Bridge

The metal panelling on the walls throughout this station give it a modern yet industrial feel. It's a big station with plenty of tunnels, stairs and escalators to entertain any photographer for a good while.

Gants Hill

Gants Hill is on the Central line quite a long way out of central London, but it has a beautiful art deco interior. In the main concourse you'll find a delicate barrel–vaulted ceiling, old–fashioned platform clocks and round uplighters gently illuminating the scene. (If you're into art deco another good station is Southgate, which has some great escalators.)

Bank & Monument

These two stations are interlinked and consist of a labyrinth of tunnels. There's no particular classic shot here, but there are plenty of passageways, staircases and escalators to explore.

Westminster

The main photographic attraction in this station is the escalator hall that descends down to the Jubilee line platforms. The escalators, along with staircases and supporting beams, criss-cross the hall creating a wonderful industrial scene. It can be captured from all sorts of different angles and the abundance of stainless steel and concrete add to the stark atmosphere of the station.

There's a tube map at the back of the book for reference. Also, see page 105 for important information about taking photos on the tube.

Higher Views

If you've explored all the views in the book, but you don't mind paying for a drink or some food to investigate even more, then there are a few restaurants and bars worth visiting. Bear in mind that these aren't purpose built viewing galleries, so leave your tripod at home and be considerate to other diners. Also, be aware that they're on the expensive side and some do have dress codes, for example no flip flops or sportswear.

The Vertigo Bar at Tower 42 (www.vertigo42.co.uk)

Tower 42 (formerly known as the NatWest Tower) is the second highest skyscraper in the City area. On the top floor is a champagne bar called Vertigo 42. From here you have fabulous views west towards St Paul's and south to the Shard, and a reasonable view east past the Gherkin to Canary Wharf. Entrance is reservation–only and there's a £15 minimum spend. All the views are from behind glass, so reflections can be a problem. See their website for location, opening hours, prices and booking.

Heron Tower

Also located in the City area is Heron Tower, which has two restaurants near the top – Sushi Samba (www.sushisamba.com) and The Duck and Waffle (www.duckandwaffle.com) They both offer great views of large parts of London and there's also an outdoor terrace, which alleviates the problems that come with shooting behind glass. The only downside is that large cameras (i.e. SLRs) aren't allowed, but compacts and camera phones are fine. See their websites for the location of Heron Tower, opening hours and prices (reservations recommended).

Vista Bar (www.thetrafalgar.com/vista-homepage)

Although the Vista Bar isn't very high up it's got great views over Trafalgar Square. It's on the roof of the Trafalgar Hotel on the southwestern corner of the square (N.B. it's only open in spring and summer).

Markets

As well as the markets in the main part of the book (Camden, Borough, Leadenhall, Brick Lane and Columbia Road) here are a couple more:

Portobello Road Market (open-air) www.portobelloroad.co.uk

Portobello Road is in the fashionable area of Notting Hill in west London. It's open every day except Sunday, however the main event is on Saturday when hundreds of antiques dealers set up stalls along the road. The antiques section is at the southern end of the road – further north you'll find fruit & veg, fashion and second hand goods. See the website for opening times and details. Nearest tube stations: Notting Hill Gate (for the southern end), Ladbroke Grove (for the northern end).

Old Spitalfields Market (covered) www.oldspitalfieldsmarket.com

This is one of the oldest markets in the East End and inside you'll find a bewildering mix of bric–a–brac, fashion, gifts and art. It's open every day but the main market days are Thursday, Friday, Saturday and Sunday. Different days have different 'themes', for example Thursday is antiques day. See the website for opening hours and details. Nearest tube stations: Liverpool Street, Aldgate, Aldgate East.

Petticoat Lane Market (open-air)

This market is also in the East End, not far from Old Spitalfields. It's often described as London's biggest jumble sale, but confusingly there's no street called Petticoat Lane any more – the name was changed in 1848 to Middlesex Street. On Sundays you'll find over 1000 stalls in and around Middlesex Street that mostly sell clothes, although you'll also find things like bric–a–brac and household goods too. It's open from 9am to 3pm. There's also a smaller market on Wentworth Street that's open from Monday to Friday. Nearest tube stations: Liverpool Street, Aldgate, Aldgate East.

Greenwich Market (covered) www.greenwichmarketlondon.com

In this covered market in Greenwich you'll find food, art, crafts, antiques, fashion and lifestyle goods. It's open every day 10am – 5.30pm, but different stalls are there on different days, for example craft and design on Tuesdays, Wednesdays and weekends. See the website for details.

Churches

London is absolutely packed with beautiful churches. Here are some of the more photogenic ones that allow photography inside (N.B. photography is not allowed when services or concerts are on, or for commercial purposes). Not all of them allow tripods, so please ask before using one, and donations are always welcome. See the websites for the location and visiting times for each.

St Martin in the Fields (www.stmartin-in-the-fields.org)

St Martin in the Fields is on the northeast corner of Trafalgar Square. It has a grand neoclassical exterior with towering Corinthian columns and a delicate spire. The interior is also charming, with low-hanging chandeliers and an ornate plaster ceiling. The walls are white with a smattering of gold gilding and this contrasts really well with the dark wood pews.

St Bride's (www.stbrides.com)

This church is just off Fleet Street in the City, not far from Temple Church (see page 68). It has an interesting barrel–vaulted ceiling with oval windows and a striking black and white geometric tiled floor. As with most churches, the favoured composition here is to shoot looking straight along the nave to the altar.

St Clement Danes (www.raf.mod.uk/stclementdanes)

St Clement Danes is on the Strand, not far from Temple tube station. It's the central church for the Royal Air Force and the interior is similar in decoration to St Martin in the Fields (dark wood pews with white walls and gold gilding). There are also plenty of subjects to do details shots of here, such as coats of arms, the squadron badges inlaid in the floor and stained glass windows.

St Mary Aldermary (homepage.ntlworld.com/mothersole)

This church is also in the City (near Mansion House) and has some wonderful Victorian stained glass windows that are great to do close–up detail shots of, but it's the gothic fan–vaulted ceiling that's the main attraction. There's an exquisite level of detail in the plaster work and the white colour scheme shows it off perfectly.

St Stephen Walbrook (ststephenwalbrook.net)

Just a few minutes' walk from St Mary Aldermary is St Stephen Walbrook. This is another church with contrasting dark wood pews and white walls, but is different from many of the others in that it has a beautiful domed ceiling. The dome is supported by Corinthian columns and the church has a light and airy feel. A popular composition here is to shoot the dome looking straight up from the altar.

Highgate Cemetery (www.highgatecemetery.org)

This atmospheric cemetery in north London is a delight to explore with a camera. There is an entrance fee, but it's worth it for the intricately carved gravestones and tombs that have been shrouded over time by ivy and lichen. You're free to roam around the East Cemetery, but access to the West Cemetery with the grander tombs is by guided tour only.

Westminster Cathedral (www.westminstercathedral.org.uk)

Westminster Cathedral (not to be confused with Westminster Abbey, see page 20) is the seat of the Roman Catholic church in England. While the outside of the building isn't to everyone's taste, the inside has some hidden gems. The Lady Chapel is especially stunning, with marble walls and a gold mosaic decorated ceiling.

Parks & Gardens

Kew Gardens (www.kew.org)

Situated on the banks of the Thames, ten miles west of central London, is the Royal Botanic Gardens at Kew. It's one of the finest gardens in the world, with everything from waterlilies to cacti and orchids, so a must-visit location if you're into botanical photography. It covers a huge 300 acres and different areas are best at different times of year, for example the woods surrounding Queen Charlotte's Cottage are carpeted in bluebells in the spring and the Arboretum is a good bet for rich golden colours in the autumn. To focus your efforts, when buying your ticket just ask which areas are particularly good at the minute. Interesting locations to photograph at any time of year are the pagoda in the southeast corner, the dutch-style Kew Palace and the Palm House, which is a beautiful Victorian glasshouse. Full details of how to get to Kew, along with a map of the site, can be found on their website.

Richmond Park (www.royalparks.org.uk)

Richmond Park is about 15 miles southwest of central London. It's the largest of the Royal Parks at over 2000 acres and is a mixture of meadows and woodland. It's one of the best places in the UK to photograph red and fallow deer. The best season to photograph the deer is autumn when the 'rut' (breeding season) is in full swing, although they can be seen at any time of year. To get a really atmospheric shot head there for sunrise on a misty morning. Be careful not to get too close to the deer (no closer than 50 metres), especially during the rut as the stags can be aggressive. As the deer are free to roam the park there's no single place you are guaranteed or more likely to see them. The best idea is to get to the park in the most convenient way for you then head towards Pen Ponds in the centre. During the rut listen out for the bellows from the stags, which will help you find them. Another good photographic subject in the park is Isabella Plantation, which is an interesting landscaped woodland garden that's best visited in the spring.

Hyde Park & Kensington Gardens (www.royalparks.org.uk)

Hyde Park and adjoining Kensington Gardens make up the largest green space in central London. Here you'll find the Serpentine (a man-made boating lake), ornamental flower beds and tree lined avenues. The whole park is a delight to roam around, but particular points of photographic interest are Serpentine Bridge (roughly in the middle of the park), the Italian Gardens (at the northern tip of the Serpentine) and the Sunken Garden at Kensington Palace (at the western edge, which is free to visit). The Italian Gardens is actually a water garden, with four fountains surrounded by delicate iron railings and ornate stone balustrades. There's a good viewpoint from the Tazza Fountain (the one with the statues and urns either side) looking down the Serpentine with the fountain in the foreground.

Holland Park

This small park in the West London borough of Kensington & Chelsea contains a beautiful Japanese garden called Kyoto Garden. Here you'll find elegant Japanese shrubs and trees, a pond complete with stepping stones and even a small cascading waterfall. It's at its best in spring and in the autumn when the trees turn golden. The park is also home to various wildlife including some peacocks. It's open all year from 7.30am until 30 minutes before dusk.

Regent's Park (www.royalparks.org.uk)

Regent's Park, in northwest London, hosts two formal gardens worth a visit – Queen Mary's Gardens in the south and the Avenue Gardens in the south east corner. Queen Mary's Gardens are famed for their huge collection of roses (the largest in London) and the Avenue Gardens contain tiered fountains and ornamental bowls overflowing with flowers. The best time to visit is in early summer when everything is in full bloom.

Christmas Lights

Christmas is a great time to visit London as pretty much everywhere is draped in festive lights (usually from mid November until the end of December). Particularly good displays are found in the main shopping areas – Bond Street, Regent Street, Oxford Street, Carnaby Street and Covent Garden. There's also a huge Christmas fair in Hyde Park called Winter Wonderland (free entry). There's a particularly good viewpoint of it at night from the western side of the Serpentine, with the fair rides reflected in the water. Various ice skating rinks also pop up around London during the festive period – those at the Natural History Museum and Somerset House have the best backdrop for photos. For something a little bit different try the Enchanted Woodlands at Syon Park to the west of London (near Kew Gardens). At Christmas they light up a mile long route through the woods with a kaleidoscope of colours. See www.enchantedwoodland.com for details.

Open House Weekend

For one weekend every year in September it's possible to explore some of London's best buildings that are normally closed to the general public. It's completely free and there are hundreds to choose from. Some you have to pre-book but others you can just turn up on the day (go early as there can be considerable queues for the most popular buildings). See www.londonopenhouse.org for details. Here are some locations I'd recommend:

- **Lloyd's Building** – The spectacular central atrium of this building is a fantastic piece of architecture and a delight to photograph.
- **City Hall** – The stunning helical staircase inside City Hall is a photographer's dream. It runs the full height of the building and can be captured from all sorts of different angles.
- **The Gherkin** – Great for marvellous views over the city.
- **St Pancras Renaissance Hotel** – This refurbished Victorian hotel is beautiful on the outside but spectacular on the inside. The interior is lavishly decorated and has a remarkable main staircase. They also do tours throughout the year – £20 per person, phone 020 8241 6921 to book.
- **The Foreign and Commonwealth Office** – For grand staircases, fabulously opulent ceilings and the beautiful Durbar Court covered courtyard.
- **Channel 4 Headquarters or 88 Wood Street** – Interesting modern architecture from the same architect that designed the Lloyd's Building.

Be aware that some buildings accessible during Open House Weekend don't allow photography (e.g. The Bank of England) and some don't allow tripods, although they can usually be left with security while you go inside.

Taking Photos on the Tube

Photography for personal use is allowed on the tube while you're passing through a station (if you want to spend considerable time in a station it's best to apply for a photography permit – see www.tfl.gov.uk/filming). The same is true for train stations and DLR stations. Allowing personal photography is entirely at the station's discretion though, so if you're asked to stop please do. Also, not loitering for too long in one place and not causing an obstruction generally reduces the likelihood of being moved on by station staff. Tripods and flash photography are not allowed anywhere on the tube network or in train/DLR stations. Unsurprisingly, tube stations are usually pretty dark so you'll need to have steady hands to get sharp photos – increasing the ISO on your camera helps a lot. I'd highly recommend avoiding the morning and evening rush hours (7.30–9.30am and 4.30–7pm) – not only will you likely cause an obstruction while you try to take photos, but you'll find it extremely tricky to get shots without anybody in them.

Helpful Tips

The Weather

The UK has a reputation for being wet, but it doesn't rain as much in London as you might think and it's often short–lived. Also, believe it or not, but rain is your friend when it comes to photography in London – the reflections you get create a host of new photo opportunities, especially in places such as Piccadilly Circus and Trafalgar Square.

If it's truly terrible weather and you don't want to risk getting your camera wet then there are also plenty of places to photograph inside, such as the Natural History Museum, the British Museum, the Tate art galleries, the covered markets (such as Borough Market) and the underground stations.

Dealing with Security Staff

There are a lot of security guards in London for obvious reasons, and taking photographs can attract their attention, especially if you're using a tripod or you look like you're photographing building entrances or security measures. It's not uncommon to be approached by them and asked what you are doing or be told to stop.

The best tactic is to politely explain what you're doing and they may leave you alone. Alternatively, they may tell you to stop taking photos there. Whether they are within their rights to ask you to stop taking photos depends on whether you are on private property or public property. The general rule is that if you're on private property they can stop you, but if you're standing on public property they can't.

The problem that you're usually faced with is that it's not easy to tell whether you are in fact on public or private property – you'd be surprised how many places in London are actually private property, for example Tower Bridge, Canary Wharf, Trafalgar Square, parts of the South Bank and all the Royal Parks. If you end up in this situation you can ask them to show you where the private/public boundary is and then move onto the public area, as it's fine to photograph private property from public property (apart from a few exceptions, usually defence buildings). If this fails then the best thing to do is walk away and find something else to photograph. Being polite and smiling while dealing with them generally helps a lot. If you're asked to stop taking photos by the police it's a very good idea to cooperate regardless of whether you're on private or public property!

Commercial Photography

For the vast majority of places in London you'll need to have a permit to take photos for commercial use. Information about how to apply for a permit can usually be found on the location's website and you will usually be charged a fee.

Sunrise & Sunset Times

To get great shots you need great light, and the best light is around sunrise and sunset. The first hour of light after sunrise is known as 'the golden hour', as is the last hour of light before sunset — during these times the light is warmer and more diffused. It's usually worth staying for a while after sunset too, as you can get backlit clouds. Here are the sunrise and sunset times for London:

	Sunrise	Sunset		Sunrise	Sunset
January 1st	8.05	16.02	July 1st	4.48	21.20
January 14th	8.00	16.19	July 14th	5.01	21.11
February 1st	7.38	16.49	August 1st	5.25	20.47
February 14th	7.15	17.13	August 14th	5.46	20.23
March 1st	6.43	17.42	September 1st	6.14	19.45
March 14th	6.14	18.04	September 14th	6.35	19.16
April 1st	6.33	19.34	October 1st	7.02	18.36
April 14th	6.04	19.56	October 14th	7.24	18.08
May 1st	5.30	20.24	November 1st	6.55	16.32
May 14th	5.08	20.45	November 14th	7.18	16.11
June 1st	4.47	21.09	December 1st	7.45	15.54
June 14th	4.42	21.19	December 14th	7.59	15.51

The Sun rises in the east in the morning and sets in the west in the evening, but there are seasonal variations in the exact direction. The diagram at the top of the next page shows sunrise and sunset directions for different months of the year. To figure out how the light will behave at your chosen location use the diagram in combination with a map. There are also a few apps available to help you figure out lighting conditions, such as the Photographer's Ephemeris.

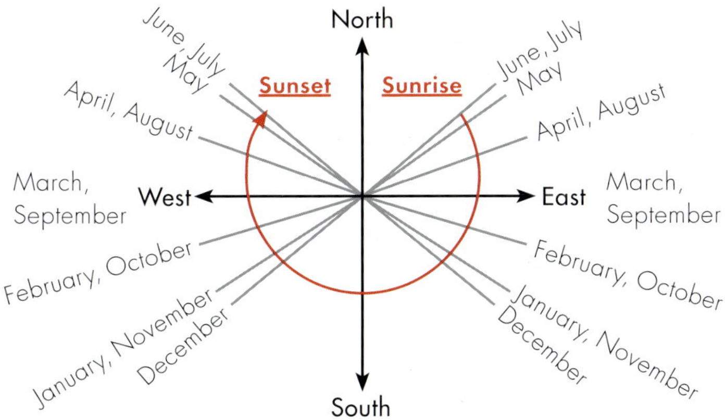

Night Photography

London is a wonderful city to photograph at night as pretty much everything is lit up. So wherever you go you're sure to find an interesting scene to photograph, whether it's a skyscraper, bridge or old building. Having said that, particularly good areas for night–time photography are the docklands and along the south bank of the Thames.

To shoot at night requires long exposures, so you'll need a tripod to steady your camera. If you don't have a tripod try to improvise one, for example balance your camera on a wall, railing or bench (although don't leave it unattended or risk it ending up at the bottom of the Thames!). Also, if you're using a compact camera and it has a night setting, then switch that on to get the best results.

One of the best times to do night photography is in what's called "blue hour". This is the hour after the Sun has completely set below the horizon. During this time indirect light from the Sun is scattered through the atmosphere and turns the sky a beautiful deep blue (after the blue hour is over the sky goes completely black). It's a particularly good time for photography as the dark blue sky contrasts well with the city lights and you generally get more definition in your photos. The effect is best when the skies are clear, but it's still a good time to photograph even with cloud cover. There's also a blue hour before the sun rises, although you'll have to get up very early to catch this. The main tourist areas in London are generally considered safe at night, although be sensible and keep an eye on your belongings.

Location Summary Table

Tripods Allowed? = A lot of places in London unfortunately don't allow tripods. You're free to use a tripod outside in public places, but be aware that you may attract attention from security guards (see page 106 for more).

Admission Fee? = This is for the area you photograph, not necessarily the location itself. For example, Westminster Abbey is listed as "no admission fee" in the table as it can only be photographed from the outside (there is an admission fee to go inside the abbey).

Photographic Interest = * good only in perfect conditions or a small range of photographic subjects, * * * * good in most conditions or has a variety of different photographic subjects.

	Location	Type of Location	Admission Fee?	Tripods Allowed?	Photographic Interest
1	Royal Albert Hall	Architecture	No	Yes	*
2	Natural History Museum	Architecture, Interiors	No	Not inside	* * * *
3	Albert Bridge	Bridge	No	Yes	* *
4	Battersea Power Station	View	No	Yes	* * *
5	Tate Britain	Interiors	No	No	* * * *
6	Westminster Abbey	Architecture	No	Not inside	* *
7	Buckingham Palace	Architecture, Changing of the Guard	No	Yes	* *
8	St James's Park	View	No	Yes	*
9	Horse Guards Parade	Changing of the Guard	No	Yes	* * *
10	Trafalgar Square	Architecture	No	Yes	* * * *
11	Piccadilly Circus	Street Scenes	No	Yes	*
12	Chinatown	Street Scenes	No	Yes	*
13	Covent Garden	Street Photography	No	Yes	*
14	The British Museum	Interiors	No	Not inside	* * * *
15	The Brewer Staircase	Spiral Staircase	No	Yes	* * *

	Location	Type of Location	Admission Fee?	Tripods Allowed?	Photographic Interest
16	Baker Street Tube Station	Tube Station	No	No	**
17	Primrose Hill	View	No	Yes	*
18	Camden Market	Street Photography	No	No	*
19	King's Cross Station	Train Station	No	No	***
20	The Houses of Parliament & Big Ben	Architecture	No	Yes	****
21	Leake Street Graffiti Tunnel	Graffiti	No	Yes	**
22	The London Eye	View	Yes to go on the Eye	Not on the Eye	****
23	Southbank Skate Park	Graffiti	No	Yes	*
24	The View From Waterloo Bridge	View	No	Yes	***
25	The View From the Oxo Tower	View	No	Yes	*
26	Southwark Tube Station	Tube Station	No	No	***
27	The Millennium Bridge	Bridge	No	Yes	****
28	Tate Modern	View, Street Photography	No	No	*
29	Southwark Cathedral	Interiors	Photo permit fee	Yes	***
30	Borough Market	Market, Street Photography	No	No	**
31	The View From The Shard	View	Yes	No	***
32	City Hall & More London	Architecture	No	Yes	****
33	Tower Bridge	Bridge	No	Yes	****
34	Temple Church	Interiors	Yes	Yes for a fee	**
35	St Paul's Cathedral	Architecture	No	Yes	****

	Location	Type of Location	Admission Fee?	Tripods Allowed?	Photographic Interest
36	The View From St Paul's	View	Yes	No	* * * *
37	The View From The Monument	View	Yes	Yes if it's not busy	* *
38	The Sky Garden	View	No	No	* * *
39	The Gherkin	Architecture	No	Yes	* *
40	The Lloyd's Building	Architecture	No	Yes	* * *
41	Leadenhall Market	Interior	No	Yes	* *
42	St Dunstan in The East	Church Ruins	No	Yes	*
43	The Tower of London	Architecture	No	Yes	* *
44	Brick Lane	Graffiti, Street Photography	No	Yes	* * *
45	Columbia Road Flower Market	Market	No	Yes	* * *
46	Canary Wharf	Architecture	No	Yes	* * * *
47	Poplar DLR Bridge	Bridge	No	No	*
48	Greenwich Foot Tunnel	Tunnel	No	Yes	* * *
49	Old Royal Naval College	Architecture, Interiors	No	No	* * * *
50	The Tulip Stairs	Spiral Staircase	No	No	* * *
51	Greenwich Park	View	No	Yes	*
52	The O2 Arena	View	Yes for cable car	Yes	*
53	Royal Victoria Dock	View	No	Yes	* *
54	The Thames Barrier	View	No	Yes	* * *

Acknowledgements

p8 top © Grant Rooney/Travel Pictures Ltd, p8 bottom © Ron Ellis/Shutterstock.com, p9 top © Scott Baldock (scottbaldockphotography.co.uk), p9 bottom © E Bowness, p10 © Yen Baet (www.yenbaet.com), p11 © Umbreen Hafeez (www.facebook.com/RealLondonPhotos), p12 top © threebythree/Shutterstock.com, p12 bottom © Frank Herrmann/fhmedien.de, p18 © E Bowness, p197 top © Umbreen Hafeez (www.facebook.com/RealLondonPhotos), p19 bottom © E Bowness, p20 top © lillisphotography/iStock, p20 bottom © Sue Martin (www.suemartin.co.uk), p21 © Umbreen Hafeez (www.facebook.com/RealLondonPhotos), p22 © Vito_Elefante/iStock, p23 © D.Godliman (www.dgphotos.co.uk), p24 © Loop Images Ltd/Alamy, p25 © Aubrey Stoll, p26 top © rabbit75_ist/Istock, p26 bottom © drnadig/Istock, p27 © Maurice Lim Wan Xiong, p28 Yen Baet (www.yenbaet.com), p29 top afotoshop/Shutterstock.com, p29 bottom Travelpix Ltd/Getty Images, p30 © Maria K Steinsson (www.mariaksteinsson.com), p31 © Lizzie Shepherd, www.lizzieshepherd.com (reproduced with kind permission from Heal's, 196 Tottenham Court Road, London W1T 7LQ heals.co.uk 0207 896 7451), p35 top © N Berry, p35 bottom © littlesam/Shutterstock.com, p36 © Andrea Pucci/Getty Images, p37 © Michael Thomas Atkinson, p38 top Alphotographic/Istock, p38 bottom Joseph Pearson Images, p39 Umbreen Hafeez (www.facebook.com/RealLondonPhotos), p44 © S.Borisov/Shutterstock.com, p45 © Matt Parry (www.mattparryphotography.com), p46 © andykirby79/iStock, p47 © WK Cheoh, p48 top Umbreen Hafeez (www.facebook.com/RealLondonPhotos), p48 bottom PhenomArtlover/Istock, p49 © Vulture Labs, p50 © Dan Breckwoldt/Shutterstock.com, p51 © Nomadic Vision Photography, p52 © Niels Stolte, p53 © Drew Buckley (www.drewbuckleyphotography.com), p54 top © TomasSereda/iStock, p54 bottom © Dan Breckwoldt/Shutterstock.com, p55 © Brian Naughton (http://naughton.photo), p56 © N Berry (reproduced with kind permission from the Chapter of Southwark Cathedral), p57 © E Bowness, p58 © Songquan Deng/Shutterstock.com, p59 © Barry Maylam (wightlandscapes.co.uk), p60 © David Kittos Photography (IG: @dck_photography), p61 © 2014 Paul Shears www.paulshearsphotography.com, p62 © Jordan | Photo, p68 © Vulture Labs (reproduced with kind permission from Temple Church), p69 top © Yen Baet (www.yenbaet.com), p69 bottom © Umbreen Hafeez (www.facebook.com/RealLondonPhotos), p70 © Otto Berkeley, p71 © Ghene Snowdon (www.gsnowdon.com), p72 Otto Berkeley, p73 © Mark "Jet" Nepomuceno, p74 top © valeriebarry/IStock, p74 bottom © Elena Elisseeva/123rf.com, p75 © coldsnowstorm/iStock, p76 © Philip Bird LRPS CPAGB/Shutterstock.com, p77 © James Charlick (www.jamescharlick.com), p78 Yen Baet (www.yenbaet.com), p79 © Umbreen Hafeez (www.facebook.com/RealLondonPhotos), p80 © E Bowness, p86 top Sean Batten (www.seanbatten.com), p86 bottom © Andrei Nekrassov/Shutterstock.com, p87 © Scott Baldock/Getty Images, p88 © Aaron Yeoman (www.aaronyeomanphotography.co.uk), p89 © Vulture Labs, p90 © Yen Baet (www.yenbaet.com), p91 © D.Godliman (www.dgphotos.co.uk), p92 top © Andrea Liu, p92 bottom © Yen Baet (www.yenbaet.com), p93 © E Bowness, p94 © Christopher Hope-Fitch/Getty Images, p95 © Umbreen Hafeez (www.facebook.com/RealLondonPhotos), p96 and p97 Yen Baet (www.yenbaet.com), p98 ©Andy Wager (www.awphotography.co.uk). With thanks to Encompass Graphics Ltd (www.encompass-graphics.co.uk) for help with the mapping.

Index

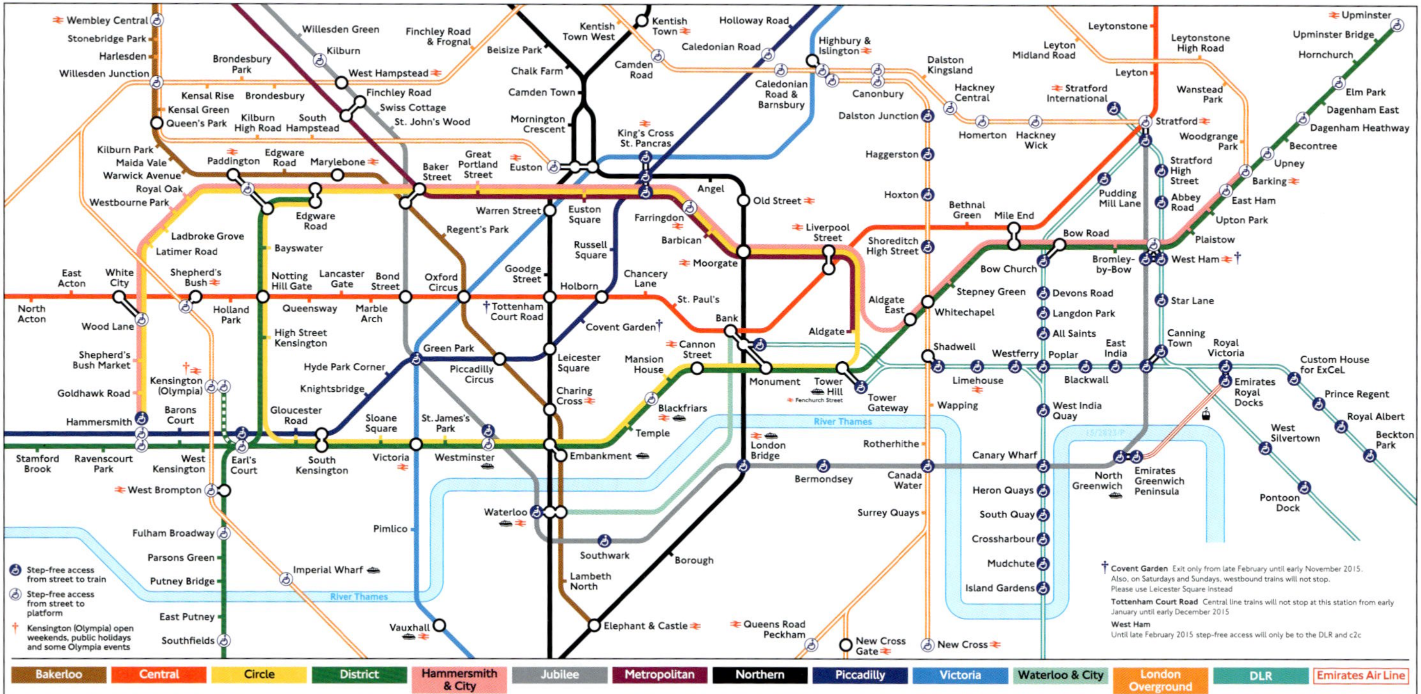

MAYOR OF LONDON

tfl.gov.uk

24 hour travel information
0343 222 1234*

*Service and network charges may apply. See tfl.gov.uk/terms for details.

Sign up for email updates
tfl.gov.uk/emailupdates

@TfLTravelAlerts

UNDERGROUND

TRANSPORT FOR LONDON
EVERY JOURNEY MATTERS

   Reg. user No. 15/2823/P   Version D 12.2014   Improvement works may affect your journey, please check before you travel   Correct at time of going to print